Michael Twomey

Grass Roots in an African City

**Grass Roots in an African City:
Political Behavior in Nairobi**

Marc Howard Ross

The MIT Press
Cambridge, Massachusetts
and London, England

This book was set in Linotype Baskerville
by Publishers' Composition Service, Inc.,
printed on Mohawk Neotext Offset,
and bound in Columbia Millbank Vellum MBV-4322
by The Colonial Press Inc.
in the United States of America

Library of Congress Cataloging in Publication Data

Ross, Marc Howard.
  Grass roots in an African city.
  Includes bibliographical references and index.
  1. Nairobi—Politics and government.   2. Nairobi—
Social conditions.   3. Political participation—
Nairobi.   I. Title.
JS7648.9.N32R66   1975   301.5′92′0967625   74-34263
ISBN   0-262-18074-X

To Jennie and Aaron

Contents

Preface

This study is an effort to bridge some of the differences between an area studies orientation and more general, theoretical social science interests. It combines aspects of both approaches and is based on the belief that both are needed to produce meaningful results. In methodological terms, the area studies approach has been excessively concerned with problems of reliability and has shown very little interest in questions of validity, while contemporary social science sometimes suffers from the opposite problem. In particular, it seems to me that the area studies people are right when they insist that meaningful statements cannot be made about a culture without the sort of immersion most associated with social anthropology, but they then fail in refusing to utilize their understanding to build meaningful generalizations. The social scientist often scoffs at their deep involvement in a culture, but without it there is often no basis for interpreting particular findings in theoretical terms.

Data presented here come from two major sources: participant observation during three field trips to Nairobi between 1966 and 1970, with the longest stay between July 1967 and March 1968, and interviews with 498 residents in two of Nairobi's housing estates, conducted in December 1967. Residents in only two neighborhoods were interviewed rather than a random sample drawn from the entire city because, at the time, we were also conducting participant observation in the two areas and felt that the better we knew the communities from which the survey data were drawn, the easier the eventual interpretation of the data would be. As our analysis proceeded, the samples from the two areas were pooled and our emphasis moved away from neighborhood differences. This occurred because it became increasingly clear that neighborhoods are more places where one happens to sleep than meaningful social units in Nairobi. Thus, an analysis that focused too much attention on neighborhood differences would be reifying these areas and would, in the end, be relying on a spurious variable for explanation.

The purpose of this short discussion of our sample in the preface is not so much methodological as an example of how the resolution of theoretical and methodological questions can depend upon detailed knowledge of the setting in which the social scientist is working. Un-like anthropology, political science has no "field work" tradition, no emphasis on language learning; in short, we often send people overseas with little more than a letter or two of introduction to high administrative officials or university contacts.

The area studies tradition is hardly a useful substitute, however. How many studies of politics in Africa ever helped increase our understanding of political life in general? How many single country studies of nation building during the preindependence period are worth reading today for anything more than historical trivia? Very few, because so many political scientists never even tried developing theoretical generalizations about political behavior. They saw their primary purpose as descriptive, and even when it was clear that comparative politics was becoming more analytic, concepts began to appear in their work more as chapter headings than as analytic tools.

To the extent that our own efforts to achieve reliability and validity have been successful, we need to acknowledge assistance from a number of sources. The Council for Intersocietal Studies at Northwestern University paid for two of the field trips to Nairobi, as well as the costs of the interviews, their coding, and key punching. The people of Nairobi, most of whom I never knew by name, communicated feelings of openness and genuine warmth. They made doing research enjoyable, if not easy, and made me want to understand better the dynamics of politics in their city. In particular, W. Gitau Gachukia, Charles Imbwaka, and Arthur Opot assisted me throughout my stay in Kenya, and I shall never forget their friendship. Ken McVicar and Andrew Hake generously taught me much of what they knew about the city of Nairobi. Peter Gutkind shared his great knowledge of urban communities in a most unselfish way, while Beatrice and John Whiting shared their enthusiasm for social science research. At Northwestern, the late David Minar encouraged me to ask basic questions about the relationship between social life and politics in Nairobi and aided me with the data analysis when it was first presented to him as a dissertation in 1968. Jack Berry, Ronald Cohen, Scott Greer, and John Paden all helped me to cope with the problem of relating field work to data analysis. Rae Moses got me started speaking Swahili. During the writing of the manuscript Remi Clignet, Roger Cobb, and Charles

Elder all gave me long detailed comments. I greatly profited from conversations with Tom Weisner, Krishna Sondhi, and Gary Ferraro about Nairobi. Danelli Holt drew the map of Nairobi. Most important, however, is the help I received from my wife Jennie-Keith, who took countless hours away from her own research and writing to help with numerous theoretical puzzles, data analysis, and proofreading. Without her this manuscript would be considerably weaker. Mrs. Marie Burtenshaw typed and retyped the manuscript with her usual goodwill and precision.

Sections of Chapter 6 appeared in "Two Styles of Political Participation in an African City," *American Journal of Political Science,* 17 (February 1973), pp. 1–22.

Marc Howard Ross
Bryn Mawr College
Bryn Mawr, Pennsylvania

Chapter 1 Political Behavior in Nairobi

Introduction

Politics in Africa has moved rapidly from the dramatic excitement of
the personalities and public events of the preindependence period to
the more mundane, routinized job of governing. It has left the fair
grounds and the meeting halls for government offices and council
chambers. In retrospect, organizing a nationalist movement capable of
attaining political independence from a somewhat weary colonial
power was far easier than the task of producing economic development
and ordered social change.

While the changes in African politics are most noticeable at the elite
level, there have also been important shifts for the majority of the
population. The mass public, mobilized for the independence struggle, responded with attendance at political rallies, votes, and even
money, in support of their expectations of almost utopian changes
promised as fruits of independence. Soon after, widespread participation in national politics diminished as the independence movement
became superfluous.

Attitudes toward politics and politicians after independence also
began to change. A growing cynicism and skepticism were fed by de-
velopments in the postindependence period. There is often dissatisfac-
tion with the progress the government has made in meeting demands
for social change and improvements in living standards, due partially
to an oversimplified view of development that many people hold, and
partially to the overly optimistic promises politicians made while
searching for votes in the preindependence period. Second, there has
been a noticeable resurgence of rivalries and conflicts between leaders
and ethnic groups that were muted during the independence struggle,
often accompanied by violence and severe repression. Third, there is
an increasingly wide gulf between a small elite, including the politicians, and the masses. Corruption is a widespread and serious problem, and there is a strong belief that politicians abuse their positions
and achieve immense personal gain at a time when they continue to
call upon the people to make sacrifices necessary to achieve development. Last, and most important, in country after country, no matter
how successful the rate of economic growth, no matter how great the

increase in secondary-school places or jobs, the provision of services has never risen as quickly as the aspiration level of the population.

All of these changes are most readily observed in the large cities in Africa. They are not only the centers of decision making and economic power but also are the only places in most countries which are ethnically and culturally heterogeneous. The residents of African cities tend to be more interested and informed about politics and to participate at a higher rate than their rural counterparts. The city means great diversity in a small area, as there are people with a wide variety of backgrounds, life-styles, and political beliefs.

In African cities today not everyone is alienated from politics, just as everyone did not actively participate in the independence movement earlier. Participation and alienation are variables whose parameters are known only generally, and whose further delineation and interrelationship are crucial to the development of propositions and theories about political behavior in a comparative context. These two general concepts provide a framework for the organization of this study of the patterns of political attitudes and activities among the mass public in an African city after independence. The concepts of political participation and political alienation need to be understood as part of the relationship between politics and the social context in which it takes place. What kinds of people are most likely to become active in political life as the independence movement loses its importance? What groups in the population will be most disaffected? How does the emergent class structure influence political behavior? Will tribal differences be more important than those of social class, sex, or urban experience in explaining political attitudes? How do people perceive changes in living conditions since independence, or the importance of tribalism and corruption as political problems?

POLITICAL BEAHVIOR

Politics in Africa, as elsewhere, is most often discussed from the perspective of elites and activists. Politics is also important to other members of a society, as it affects virtually all members of a community. While not denying the importance of the actions and feelings of political leaders in shaping the futures of citizens or African nations, this study begins from an alternative starting point. It asks how average citizens look at politics in their society, the ways in which they do or do not participate in political processes, and most important, it seeks to understand the social forces that account for variation in political beliefs and behaviors in an African city. While the study of political behavior from the perspective of the average citizen is not new in the social sciences, there remain a large number of questions whose answers are unclear.

One important problem that can be understood only if researchers begin to study mass as well as elite behavior is the ways in which mass attitudes and actions shape the character and conduct of the elites and vice versa. While democratic theorists have discussed for a long time the various forms this relationship can take, their work has focused on theoretical desiderata not empirical relationships. What are the ways in which the mass constrains and shapes the political elite, and how does the political elite mobilize and at times manipulate the public?

A second unresolved question is the extent to which empirical findings and theoretical concepts developed in one cultural setting are likely to be generalizable to other contexts. Most studies of political behavior, for example, have been undertaken in North American or other industrial settings, and we still are uncertain whether our theories will have to be modified in light of studies in different settings or on the other hand whether we can claim a wider generality for them.

A third basic problem is the understanding of how social conditions in a society affect the character of its politics. What are the ways in which social borders between individuals provide a basis for differential political interest, involvement, and orientations to government? We need to consider more carefully how membership and participation in different social classes, ethnic groups, and life-styles shape a person's political experiences. Identification of basic relationships between social life and politics is only a start, however. It is even more important to explain the mechanisms underlying these relationships.

Our choice of an African city as a setting to consider these questions allows us to confront most directly the need for cross-cultural empirical generalizations about politics. In particular, it requires us to state from the outset that we are not so much interested in discovering whether or not Nairobi and the two neighborhoods studied intensively are somehow "typical" of Kenya, Africa, or Third World cities. Clearly, there are ways in which Nairobi is similar to other places in the world and different in others. Enumerating these is not our primary concern. We are more interested in the generalizability of our findings about the *relationships between variables* than in the description of any particular one. Then, once relationships have been identified, it is crucial to try to learn what are the mechanisms underlying them and how these mechanisms vary cross-culturally.

This study of political behavior in Nairobi is aimed at explaining the social bases of political involvement and attitudes toward politicians and government in the postindependence period. Before going on to introduce the reader to the city and the ways in which mass political behavior was studied there, a short discussion of the major concepts is necessary.

Political participation refers to behaviors that either directly or indirectly attempt to influence decision making in any society.[1] It is concerned not only with overtly political acts, such as joining a political party or voting, which are usually supportive of existing political institutions (if not politicians), but also with the kinds of actions that individuals undertake to reshape or replace existing political structures. An inquiry into political participation in postindependence Africa, then, is concerned with the ways in which the mass public shapes political outcomes. It must ask what kind of political activities people engage in and also distinguish types of people who are likely to be politically involved from those who are unconcerned with politics.

Political attitudes considered here are mass beliefs about Kenya's politicians and government. We learn how people evaluate the performance of the government since independence as well as the presence of feelings of political alienation, which is defined in terms of *political estrangement and political powerlessness*.[2] Political estrangement is an individual's belief that the present political authorities are unable or unwilling to serve the interests of people like himself, while political powerlessness is the belief that an individual has little or no control over or input into the political decision making process in his community or society. Estrangement focuses the feelings of alienation on politicians and political institutions, while powerlessness indicates an individual's feelings about his own political capabilities. An important question also considered is how these different behaviors and beliefs are related to one another as well as to the social context in which they occur.

Political participation and alienation are the major phenomena to be explained in this study. We are interested in identifying variables associated with different levels of these behaviors and attitudes across individuals in the city. As the major explanatory concepts, we will employ social status, life-style, and ethnicity, three basic elements of social organization in urban settings.[3] Each of these is hypothesized to affect political orientations and involvement independently in the following manner.

Social status markers, such as literacy or wealth, represent resources that individuals can devote to politics. The overwhelming evidence from studies in diverse, although primarily western settings, is that the higher an individual's social status, the more active in political life and the more informed about politics that person is likely to be.[4] Furthermore, social status is positively related to the presence of feelings of political efficacy. Increased involvement, however, does not necessarily mean participation in activities supportive of the current regime or political authorities. Thus, increases in social status are associated with increases in political participation, while the forms that such participation takes and the goals aimed at are dependent upon additional conditions. Part of our task is the identification of these additional elements in Nairobi where, for example, the highly estranged in some ethnic groups are more politically active than those low on estrangement, while in others, the direction of the relationship is reversed.

Life-style represents variations in the ways individuals participate in urban life, their range of contacts in the city, and their ties to the rural areas. Many city residents maintain strong ties to their rural families and view their stay in the city in highly instrumental terms. Frequently, a man migrates to the city while his wife and children remain home on the land engaging in small-scale agriculture. They may live together only during the man's vacation and between planting seasons. In other cases, individuals make a stronger commitment to city life, moving to Nairobi with their entire families. Full-time residence in the city does not mean that individuals necessarily sever rural ties, however. In fact, the strength of ties to rural families is a function of social status, as those individuals most able to pay for travel and keeping up the ties do so. The political consequences of this complex situation are not straightforward, as we shall see. Of crucial importance are the reference groups that individuals use in making judgments, and consequently our evidence shows sharp differences in attitudes across individuals at different levels of interaction with their home areas in the countryside. In one ethnic group, the high rural-urban ties promote support for the government, and in another case they are tied to disapproval. Clearly, a more general mechanism needs to be identified.

The relationship between life-style choices and political participation depends initially on the way people are recruited into politics. Because we are dealing with a case where the basis for political recruitment shifted from the independence to the postindependence periods in Kenya, we have a chance to see how the relationship between life-style and participation also changed. The maintenance of a broad network of social interactions should be more important to political participation in the postindependence period than during the independence era when there was extensive mobilization by the political elite. Those individuals having the strongest ties to the rural areas, as well as the widest network of friends in the city are, in the present period, most able to learn about politics and have the greatest number of opportunities for involvement.

Ethnicity,[5] the third independent variable, is important both as a basis for political recruitment and as a source of reference groups for the development and maintenance of political attitudes. Friendship networks in Nairobi are generally homogeneous ethnically. Similarly, reactions to political events and personalities tend to be more alike within than across ethnic borders. In the postindependence period, differences between ethnic groups have tended to be more in attitudes and orientations to government, than in the level of political involvement per se.[6] To investigate this phenomenon, as well as its consequences, we will compare with particular attention the Kikuyu, Kenya's largest tribe, which is dominant in the government, and the Luo, the second largest group among whom the opposition is strongest. For prediction of political orientations in Nairobi, while ethnic differences are most noticeable and important, they are by no means the only significant ones. Particularly striking are the ways in which social status and life-style operate within ethnic groups to explain additional sources of variation.

Finally, we are interested in how political participation and aliena-tion are associated. Most commonly, the two are seen as inversely related. Support for this view depends to some extent on which dimen-sions of alienation one considers, as the relationship is more stable with powerlessness than estrangement. In the case of the latter, par-ticipation seems to be a function of social support and participation opportunities and whether or not they are consistent with attitudinal orientations. Looking at the Kikuyu and Luo, two groups with many similar social characteristics and sharply different political orienta-tions, will show the effect of intervening structural conditions on the participation-alienation relationship.

NAIROBI: THE RESEARCH SETTING

Nairobi, Kenya's capital, is located in the south central part of the country just south of the equator. A quiet administrative center with about 100,000 inhabitants after World War II, by 1970 Nairobi had a population of over 500,000, a diversified industrial economy, and the sorts of problems found in big cities throughout the world. It is a new city, in the sense that a very small proportion of the population has lived there for a long time and considers it home. It is a city of immi-grants who still maintain ties with their families in the rural areas. Ethnic and tribal identities remain strong, and these are reflected in the political coalitions and social interactions in the city.

Like most rapidly growing cities in developing countries, Nairobi is characterized by an unevenness in the effects of social change which are compressed in both space and time. There are new modern apartment buildings with fully equipped kitchens and bathrooms located next to "shantytown" squatter settlements. The residents of the first are likely to be young, well-educated bureaucrats or businessmen, while the sec-ond are filled with people able to eke out only the most marginal existence in the city. Both groups have been displaced from rural com-munities for a variety of reasons: population pressure, family rivalries, and most important, their belief in the greater opportunity for "making it" found in the modern city. Social change has touched both groups, but in the first case it is a gentle push from behind, while in the second it is more like a kick in the teeth.

Politics in Nairobi is highly personalized. It begins with President Jomo Kenyatta. People are forever wondering what he thinks about a particular problem, which other political figures are in his favor, and most significant, who will succeed him, and what will happen to Kenya after his death. One also learns that Kenyatta is not the only politician people discuss and wonder about. Within each ethnic community there are favorites, or at least individuals receiving greater attention and interest, none of whom has truly "national" backing. For the Luo it is Odinga, for the Kamba, Ngei, for the Kalenjin, arap Moi. The rumors and stories travel quickly around the city, in sharp contrast with government programs, which are sharply hampered by limited resources.

Learning about social life in Nairobi is pleasant and not difficult. People are overwhelmingly open and friendly, and a great deal of life takes place out-of-doors, as the weather is extremely mild and housing space is often cramped. Visiting different neighborhoods of the city, one soon meets a wide range of people and learns about both the physical and social heterogeneity of Nairobi. As people talk about their own experiences and as one observes the wide range of activities going on, a picture of social and political life slowly develops. Some things are easy to find out, partially because they are obvious and partially because people are very open. Others are more difficult, often because the researcher is not sure what he is looking for.

Similarly, participant observation begins to reveal questions that are not very useful or interesting either to the researcher or to the people living in the city. Whenever anyone is asked why he first came to Nairobi, the answer is invariably the same, "I came to find work and make money." Likewise, asking a man if he liked living in the city, there were one of two replies, "I am working and making money, so I like Nairobi," or, "No, I have no work, and it is expensive." Or asked where is a good part of the city to live, a typical answer is, "A good housing estate to live in is one where I can get a room." It is not so much that people do not have opinions on these questions, rather it is not immediately clear how to tap them.

Talking with and observing Nairobi residents challenge many standard assumptions about the opposition between urban and rural lifestyles. In the city people do not so much stress the differences in each setting, but rather they understand the attractions of each and try to organize their lives so they have the best of both worlds. A young man who comes to work in Nairobi is not turning his back on rural life. Rather, he is making an instrumental decision. Jobs are in the city, and if he wants money to pay the bride-price to his future wife's family or to supply his children's school fees, chances are he has to leave home to find work. Furthermore, he may have friends and relatives living in the city and is curious about their way of life. So he comes to Nairobi, stays with a relative, and eventually finds a job and place of his own. But he does not cut his rural roots. When asked if they would like to own land in the rural areas, almost 100 percent of the people in Nairobi say "Yes." It is like asking an American if he wants to have large amounts of life insurance. Of course, he would. Land ownership in the rural areas is not seen as incompatible with city life, and residents know that when they are older, or if they lose their jobs, they can always turn to the land. Meanwhile they can have their wives or other relatives plant crops every year while they stay in town.

Ethnicity is an important social characteristic of individuals in the city. Through social cues, mainly language use and physical appearance, individuals are immediately classified in one of the major ethnic groupings. As a result, certain forms of social contact and intimacy are highly determined. Most social networks are homogeneous ethnically; images of out-groups are well articulated and generally negative. Ethnicity is often considered an explanation for important social behavior. One day a murder was committed in Bahati (a Nairobi housing estate). The dead man was a hardworking Kikuyu butcher who often sold meat to several Baluhya friends of mine. They heard he was killed by a neighbor who stole the money he kept at home. In explaining the circumstances of the killing the next day, the Baluhya said, "They are Kikuyu," which was meant as a complete explanation of the motive for the murder, the manner in which he was killed, the fact that a neighbor killed him, and the man's refusal to put his money in a bank.

Observation in Nairobi begins to reveal differences as well as simi-

larities within the African population. In addition to the ethnic differences that are most dramatic, social status is an important determinant
of individual behaviors and attitudes. Individuals have well-defined
expectations of others based on markers of status such as dress, residence, and language skills. Many people who are able to speak English
do so in situations where it is not required, as a way of showing their
higher status and putting down others who are not as fluent. Status
differences are also reflected in spatial differentiation in the city as
most residential areas are homogeneous by house rent.

Early in the research, we paid a great deal of attention to most African neighborhoods in the city. After several months, however, research
became more focused on two housing estates, Shauri Moyo and Kariokor. Both are owned and managed by the Nairobi City Council, are
relatively near each other and the center of Nairobi, and are ethnically
heterogeneous. At the same time, there are striking contrasts between
them. Shauri Moyo was built in 1938 and has 170 houses each containing six single-room flats that rent for Shs. 39/— each a month.[7]
Most of its residents are working class and do not have an easy time
making ends meet in the city. Kariokor estate, opened in the mid-
1960s, is made up of twelve four-story buildings each containing twenty
spacious apartments, which rent for Shs. 240/—a month. Its inhabitants
are young, well-educated, and hold important white-collar positions in
the city.

Participant observation provided rich data about how people viewed
politics. Getting people to talk about politics, particularly about individual politicians, is not difficult. What proved to be even more important, however, were the political topics that entered into conversations without prodding. All that is necessary is to sit back and listen to
how people define political issues, perceive political leaders, and react
to them. In addition, there is also the opportunity to see how people
behave when problems arise. What do they do when they get involved
in a dispute over land ownership? when they want the city council to
repair something in their housing estate? when they couldn't raise
the money to pay school fees? Each of these sorts of cases was played
out in front of me. In each situation it was possible to observe how
people defined the issue, whom they went to for advice, and what
action they took with what result.

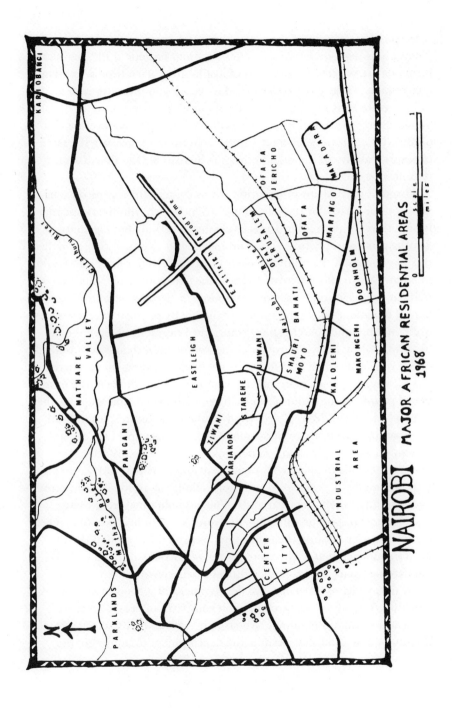

NAIROBI MAJOR AFRICAN RESIDENTIAL AREAS
1968

Despite the richness of these data, however, they are not very systematic and inadequate for hypothesis testing. For one thing, informants are selected on the basis of availability, friendliness, and language skills. Thus, more systematic data collection procedures needed to be used in conjunction with participant observation once we could define clearly the questions to be studied.[8] Through the development of multiple indicators, using different techniques to measure the same concepts, validity of the final findings is increased. One short illustration may be useful.

Through participant observation it was evident that ethnicity was an important basis for the selection of friends with whom one spent leisure time. In particular, I was struck by the ethnic homogeneity of visiting groups in people's rooms or apartments. To investigate further this phenomenon, I conducted a census in 10 percent of the households in Shauri Moyo and Kariokor to learn the extent of ethic homogeneity in marriage and household composition. Second, because the members of the major tribes are quite identifiable by physical characteristics, dress, manner and speech, an assistant and I began to observe the ethnic composition of small groups in the two neighborhoods. We walked slowly down the street at different times of day, and whenever there was a group of two or more people we noted on a code sheet the number of people in the group from each tribe, their sex, and whether they were adults or children. Third, we used the same techniques in local bars, coding the ethnic composition of drinking groups. Last, interviews were conducted with 498 persons over 18 randomly selected from households in Shauri Moyo and Kariokor. As part of the interview, respondents were asked questions about the residence and ethnic background of their closest friends. The data obtained from these different techniques provided greater confidence in making statements about ethnicity because the techniques were so different and the indicators independent.[9] The more intensive participant observation data are necessary for learning cultural categories and asking good questions, which is crucial to the development of a good interview schedule. The survey research data, in comparison, provide more superficial information about a large number of randomly selected individuals, a method that permits the development of more reliable generalizations. Used together, participant observation and survey research yield two very different but complementary forms of data.

Plan of the Book

This is a study of political behavior in Nairobi from the perspective of mass attitudes and behaviors. Part I provides a portrait of social and economic life in Nairobi at the time of the study, using the concepts of life-style, social status, and ethnicity. Part II then employs these concepts as independent variables in explaining patterns of political participation and alienation in the city. What emerges is an understanding of the ways in which politics in the postindependence period in Kenya is different than during the independence era, and how involvement in politics and orientations to government and political authorities are shaped by the social setting of the city.[10]

Part **I** Social Life in Nairobi

Chapter 2   Nairobi and Its Neighborhoods

Nairobi is strikingly new, as are many of Africa's large cities. Although there have been cities on the continent for centuries, the percentage of the population living in them, or the percentage of people whose lives were affected by them, has always been very small. The population of Nairobi has quadrupled since 1945, as centralized government activity, industrial development, and commerce expanded rapidly in the later phases of colonial rule.

Such dramatic population growth is quite typical of African cities.[1] What is equally striking, however, is the unevenness of the effects of the expansion on the city population. The modern center city areas are filled with ten- and fifteen-story buildings, drive-in parking lots, and the hustle and bustle of people going to and from work in modern offices. A few miles away there are the modern apartment buildings or even the neatly spaced new houses where the civil servants and young elite live. But this is only part of the story of change, as there are also neighborhoods, such as Shauri Moyo, where entire families are living in small single rooms, and where the men are grateful to find any employment at all because the job market is oversupplied. Here people cannot save for the future because they are hardly able to pay for the present. On a third level, there are people in the city whose existence is marginal in every sense of the term. They are unemployed squatters who have come to the city for a variety of reasons. Often they have no rural alternatives, although urban prospects are also bleak. They subsist, on a day-to-day basis, through activities such as petty commerce, illegal beer brewing, part-time labor, and prostitution.[2] All of these people are part of the urban community, but they are not all affected in the same way by the changes taking place within it.

There are, of course, a variety of ways in which one can begin to describe urban diversity. For our purposes, the concepts of ethnicity, life-style, and social status provide a useful starting point for understanding the growth and development of Nairobi and the present spatial differentiation of its population. During the early years of the twentieth century, differences on these three characteristics tended to be highly interrelated and were coterminous with racial differences among the European, Asian, and African communities. Today there are greater variation and independence in ethnicity, life-style, and social status. Our interest is in the African population of Nairobi and in eventually showing how an individual's ethnicity, life-style, and social status affect his political attitudes and behaviors.

Ethnicity and Race

Nairobi is a new African city. Prior to European penetration into Kenya the land on which the city is located today was a marshland that served as a natural border between the southern Kikuyu population of Kiambu and the Athi Plains, controlled by the Masai. Building in the city began in 1899 when the railway from Mombasa reached Nairobi.[3] The settlement initially served as a base for the railway between the coast and Lake Victoria, at the edge of the great Rift Valley. In the early years health conditions in the marshland provoked several battles over the site of the city, but the railway officials protested vigorously enough so that the site was not changed.[4] By 1906 the population was over 13,000,[5] railway and government headquarters were moved to Nairobi, and the debate concerning the town's location essentially ended.

From the outset, the population was stratified by race, and each racial tier contained numerous subdivisions. The Europeans dominated the government and larger financial institutions of the city, although they were never more than 8 or 10 percent of the population; the Asians, many of whom came to East Africa to work on the construction of the railway, were chiefly engaged in all ranges of commerce or as artisans, and made up about a quarter of the city's population; the remaining two-thirds of the residents of Nairobi were Africans who worked in the most menial occupations. The three racial groups were separated residentially and stratified socially as well as economically. For example, until the independence era, differential wage scales for the same work existed for each race in most areas of employment. The Europeans maintained firm political control, although there were often bitter conflicts between the administration and the settler community.[6]

The majority of the African population, with the exception of domestic employees working in Europan or Asian homes, resided east of the center of the town.[7] By 1910 there were six separate African settlements each of which was under the jurisdiction of its own headman.

Early government records indicate that the African population included persons from Tanzania and Uganda and members of the Kenya tribes from the coast as well as of those whose home areas are nearer Nairobi. Prominent in the early records are the Somalis, who in certain respects were accorded higher status than the rest of the African community. Swahilis,[8] often Moslems, seemed to be more numerous than they are today.

In the first decade of the century, the town's provision of social services to the African and Asian segments of the population was almost nonexistent. Just prior to the outbreak of hostilities in the 1914–1918 war, the administration began discussing the inadequacy of African housing and sanitation facilities in Nairobi and the possibility of developing a "new Native Location."[9] However, the outbreak of the war halted any incipient plans.

During the 1920s and 1930s most Africans worked in unskilled occupations such as domestic servants, porters, messengers, and so forth. In the early thirties a few began their own businesses. They started as charcoal dealers or hawkers or opened small tea hotels. These businesses required a minimal amount of capital and provided goods or services exclusively to other Africans. Some people kept domestic animals, and, in addition, maize and other crops were planted in the open fields throughout the city, and the products were either sold in the city or consumed at home. The first African dukas (shops) were opened in the 1930s. The first shops in Pumwani were either Arab or Indian owned and run, although they were mainly African by the time of independence. As part of the Shauri Moyo estate, the city council constructed a number of shops that Africans have rented since the late 1930s.

There was no great effort on the part of the government to provide primary education for the children of the Africans living in Nairobi. In fact, by 1941, there was still only one government-run school for Africans, which was located in Pumwani. The Church Missionary Society, which opened the first school, the Catholic Church, and the Salvation Army maintained the three other schools for Africans in Nairobi. The number of students in these four schools was about 1100,[10] which was less than 30 percent of the school-age population in the city.

The postwar period brought an intensification of racial animosities in Kenya and Nairobi. Many Africans served in the British armed forces in India and Burma during the war. They saw firsthand the nationalist activity in India and experienced situations of racial equality they never had seen at home. Upon their return to Kenya, Africans were disappointed and bitter to find so little change.[11] In the late 1940s ex-servicemen were prominent in new political associations and militant nationalist agitation in Nairobi.

The Europeans were unwilling even to consider sharing power at that time and tended to blame African agitation on a few troublemakers. By 1952 the Kenya government declared a State of Emergency because of the guerrilla activities of "Mau Mau" freedom fighters, and direct military action was taken against the entire African population, but in particular against members of the Kikuyu, Embu, and Meru tribes. There were a number of police raids within the city in which several thousand Kikuyus were rounded up, brought before screening committees, and then either released or sent to detention camps. Kikuyu, Embu, and Meru were moved out of Kaloleni and Ziwani housing estates to Bahati, Bondeni, and Kariokor.[12] The rights of individuals were totally ignored; in almost all cases a man could not confront his accuser or learn the nature of the evidence against him. The administration, instead, engaged in a number of capricious and arbitrary actions such as the following:

On the 26th October (1953) all Kikuyu/ Embu/ Meru tea hawkers were forbidden to trade for one month, as many of them had been witnesses to crimes, but had produced no information regarding the criminals.[13]

By the end of the decade the European power claimed to have stamped out Mau Mau, and African political activity was permitted once again. By this time political independence, rather than sharing power with a small white minority, was the goal of Kenyan activists, and all but the most die-hard white settlers in Kenya recognized the inevitability of the situation. Led by Jomo Kenyatta, after his release from detention camp, the Kenya African National Union (KANU) won the support of the major African tribal communities and led the country to independence in 1963.[14]

Since independence European-African relations have been relatively good. The independent African government has welcomed continued European participation, particularly economic, in Kenya, but at the same time insisted on final control. Asian-African relations, in contrast, have been much more problematic as the majority African community has asserted itself against a far smaller, and highly visible minority. The government has imposed restrictions on Asians and has sought to expel those who do not have Kenya citizenship. A few years after independence, it is clear to all that Kenya is to be an African country, and political participation has become a rarity for the outnumbered Europeans and Asians.

Since independence ethnic differences within the African population are of increased importance in Kenya as in a number of African nations. Some neighborhoods in Eastlands, where a majority of the African population of Nairobi lives, are ethnically distinctive. In some cases, such as Ziwani or Kaloleni, there are few Kikuyus and many Luo and Baluhya, as a consequence of the forced removal of the Kikuyu population during the Emergency. Other areas, such as Bahati and Ofafa I (Kunguni), have predominantly Kikuyu populations, for these were the areas where Kikuyus were forced to live by the government during the Emergency. Most African residential areas, however, are ethnically heterogeneous. Most housing has been built either by the government, by employers, or by private individuals (often Asians), and as a result ethnically homogeneous neighborhoods, such as one finds in other cities in Africa, are, for the most part, noticeably absent. Furthermore, because of a severe shortage, people are likely to take housing wherever they can get it and do not have the choices that might produce ethnic neighborhoods.

Ethnicity, within the African community, differentiates individuals less spatially than in terms of social and political choices. Close friends are overwhelmingly drawn from an individual's ethnic community; contact outside is often limited. There are strong stereotypes of different ethnic groups, and at times of tension, such as the assassination of the Luo Minister for Planning and Economic Development by a Kikuyu in 1969, mobilization and interaction within each ethnic community are intense.

The major African ethnic groups in Kenya are all overrepresented

Table 2.1. 1969 Population of Major Tribes in Kenya and Nairobi, Percent of Each Tribe in Kenya and Nairobi, and the Ratio of Each Tribe in the City/Nation[15]

Tribe	Population in Kenya (1)	Population in Nairobi (2)	Percent of Kenya (3)	Percent of Nairobi (4)	Percent of Kenya Africans in Nairobi (5)	Percent of Group in Nairobi (2)/(1)	Ratio of (5)/(3)
Kikuyu	2,201,632	191,367	20.1%	37.6%	46.9%	8.7%	2.33
Luo	1,521,595	62,865	13.9	12.3	15.4	4.1	1.10
Baluhya	1,453,302	65,056	13.3	12.8	15.9	4.5	1.20
Kamba	1,197,712	60,716	10.9	11.9	14.9	5.1	1.37
Other Kenyan African	4,299,529	27,732	39.3	5.4	6.9	.9	.17
Tanzania	26,360	5,261	.2	1.0	—	20.0	—
Uganda	17,232	4,854	.2	.9	—	28.2	—
Asian	139,037	67,189	1.3	13.2	—	32.1	—
European	40,593	19,185	.4	3.8	—	47.3	—
Total Kenya African Population	10,673,770	407,736	99.5%	98.9%	100.0%		
Total Population	10,942,705	509,286					

in Nairobi's population, although the urban percentage of any one ethnic group is well under ten, as shown in Table 2.1. The Kikuyu, the country's largest tribe, is also the largest group in the city, constituting almost half of Nairobi's African population. The Luo, Baluhya, and Kamba, the next three largest groups in the country, make up about one-sixth of the city's African population each. Thus, the four largest groups constitute over 90 percent of the African population of Nairobi. The only other population groups overrepresented in Nairobi's population are the foreign communities, as a very large proportion of Europeans and Asians, as well as Tanzanians and Ugandans in Kenya, is found in Nairobi.[16] No other groups are larger than 1 percent of the city's population total.

Because of the population distribution in Nairobi, a resident there can easily exaggerate the relative numerical importance of Kenya's major ethnic groups. The city's politics tends to pay little attention to other groups in the country, although their population may actually be quite large. Interactions among the major groups in the city are frequent and face to face. Contact, however, does not necessarily result in understanding and mutual attraction. In fact, in many competitive situations, interaction can reinforce distrust and suspicion, as ethnic group membership serves as the basis for the distribution of jobs, housing, and other government services in Nairobi.[17]

Life-style

Throughout the colonial period Africans viewed Nairobi as a European city. While residence in the city could be justified on instrumental grounds, relatively few Africans saw it as an attractive place. Thus, the turnover, or instability, of Nairobi's African population has been quite high over time. Only a small proportion regarded themselves primarily as city residents. Instead, the pattern has been to regard the town as a place to earn money during one's middle years and then to return to the rural areas in old age. The town was considered no place to bring a wife or raise a family. In addition, where some people might have reached a different conclusion, they were left with little choice, as the wage levels in the city were so low that it was difficult, if not impossible, to support a wife and children adequately.[18] Data from every census available in Nairobi show (1) an extremely high adult male/female ratio, and (2) an extremely high adult/child ratio.

The age and sex structure of Nairobi's African population shows the ambivalence with which city life was regarded. Length of residence in Nairobi was often short, as men returned to the rural areas when they accumulated enough money to purchase a plot of land or pay their children's school fees. Relatively few men brought their families to live with them in the city. This was quite evident in 1962 when the adult African[19] male/female ratio was 2.5:1, whereas among children the number of males and females was almost equal. In addition, the ratio of adults/children was 2.1:1 in Nairobi for Africans, while it was 1.2:1 for the Asian community in the capital and 1.2:1 in the entire nation.

This imbalance has been decreasing since the war. (In 1948 the male/female ratio for adult Africans was about 5:1, almost the same as in 1911.) However, it is still much higher than the ratio in most other cities of its size in developing nations. In Mombasa and Nakuru, the second and third largest cities in Kenya, the adult African male/female ratio was 1.5:1.[20] A consequence of the sex structure is that the 1962 census showed that only 12.8 percent of the African population were born in Nairobi, and most of these were young children.[21] Less than 5 percent of the adults living in Nairobi were born there.

Because a pattern has been established for older men to leave the city and return to the rural areas, Nairobi's African population is much more clustered by age than that of the nation as a whole. City residents are underrepresented in both the younger and older age groups and overrepresented in the middle ones—the ages when people are most likely to seek wage employment. Although only 2.5 percent of the residents in Nairobi were 55 or older in 1962, 5.8 percent of the nation exceeded this age. In Nairobi 51.1 percent were between 20 and 44; this group comprised just 31.7 percent of the national total. In the city, 40.9 percent of the population were under 20; however, in the nation they were 56.4 percent.[22]

As a result of these sex and age differences there are striking disparities in the composition of households in Nairobi and the nation at large. Residents of Nairobi have a greater tendency to live with non-relatives than people in the rest of the country. Of the Nairobi residents, 25.7 percent were not related to the head of the household, while only 4.2 percent in the rest of the country were not relatives. In addition, wives and children were less represented in Nairobi households than in the rest of Kenya. Only 39.4 percent of the residents of the city were the wife, son, or daughter of the head of household; in the nation they comprise 71.6 percent of all households. Finally, households in Nairobi tend to contain more secondary relatives than households in the country.[23]

One way in which urban-rural ties are maintained is through marriage. There are relatively few unmarried women living in the city. Thus it appears that men must find brides (often several years younger than themselves) in the rural areas and in some cases return to the city with them. Although the percentage of married women living in the city is only slightly higher than that for men—79.3 percent as opposed to 73.1 percent—the differences are greatest for the younger age groups. Of the women between 15 and 19, 61.8 percent are married; however, only 7.4 percent of the men have brides at that age. In the next age group, 20 to 24, 85.1 percent of the women are married in contrast to only 42.8 percent of the men. The figures presented differ very little from the figures for the nation. Census data show a sharp rise in the percentage of widowed, separated, or divorced women in the city in each succeeding age group. A worthwhile question to ask, which is un-answerable with the data available, is whether these women migrate into the city or whether this represents the effects of city life for a generation that was born in the rural areas of Kenya. There is no simi-lar rise in this category for men. Instead, the percentage of married men seems to level off a few percentage points above 90 percent after the age of 30.[24]

During the colonial period life-style choices were often dictated by the almost total absence of adequate housing for African families in the city.[25] For many years the concept of "bedspace" was the only one that entered into the construction of lodgings.[26] One consequence of this to Europeans was the high rate of labor turnover and the consequent low productivity. Housing conditions came to be seen by many as the root cause of African discontent in the city. For example, one report said:

Instead of the frequent return to his reserve, a desire which is only to be expected of a worker living apart from his wife, family and home life, he should stay longer, acquire a greater skill and give a greater return for his cost. Indeed we should look to the creation of a Nai-robi urban working class. The means of creating a permanent Nairobi urban native Community with its own institutions and its own sense of responsibility and communal pride exist . . . social prog-ress in Nairobi depends on more housing.[27]

Improved housing conditions, they suggested, would solve the major social problems in Nairobi. It would ensure a greater stability in the urban population of the city which would have two effects: one economic and one political. The economic effect would mean that European and Asian employers would receive a higher return on their capital expended for job training programs because the labor turn-over would decrease. The political effect would be that an impor-tant cause of the unrest and discontent of the urban population would be removed, and therefore political agitation would diminish.

The number of urbanized individuals, in the sense of those people committing themselves to city life, remained far below the number

of Africans who had had urban experience in Nairobi. Because
most men left their wives and children in the rural areas when they
came to work in the city, they tended to maintain relatively high
levels of interaction and attachment to the rural communities. Social
structures did not develop to replace those in the rural areas, rather
those institutions that were most effective in the city also served
rural goals and helped individuals maintain rural ties, as few people
could afford to cut themselves off from the countryside. Therefore,
as Rosberg and Nottingham have observed:

One inherent consequence of this low wage economy was that nearly
all African workers had to maintain an economic, social and political
stake in their own tribal areas in order to meet the minimum
requirement of subsistence and security for themselves and their
families. . . . Since workers had thus to depend on the rural areas,
the vast majority were unable to commit themselves irrevocably to
the towns. There was little hope that an independent, permanently
settled, urbanized community would develop within such an
economic system.[28]

Social Status

Until the very end of the colonial period, race served as the most
powerful indicator of social ranking in Nairobi. Although there were
always differences in education or income with each of the three
racial communities, particularly in the case of Africans, these were
always relatively small in comparison with differences across racial
groups. Since about 1960 there has been increased mobility and
social differentiation within the African community, and an African
elite based on wealth, education, and occupational position is now
clearly identifiable.

Social status is the basis for power and privilege in a society. In
Kenya, as in many developing nations, criteria such as education,
income, and occupation are the key markers of social status, as opposed to ascriptive criteria, such as family position or even age. A
high-status individual in Nairobi in the postindependence period
probably has a white-collar job that pays a good salary. He probably
has at least a secondary-school education, wears western suits, drives a
car, and speaks English.

Our interest is in the political consequences of these status differences within the African community. Two sorts of questions then

become relevant: (1) What are the skills and resources available to individuals of higher status which may become relevant in politics? Educational achievement and literacy probably help individuals to understand the operation of a relatively complicated government bureaucracy and to keep up with printed news about politics, giving them the possibility of becoming involved as the need arises. (2) A second way in which status considerations are relevant to politics is in the possibility that differences in prestige provide differential access to political and governmental authorities. To what extent does a person need to speak English and wear certain clothes to get government officials to listen to his problems and respond to them? To what extent does he need to have personal ties to politicians to achieve results? How important are class-based interpersonal friendship networks in politics?

In Nairobi, as in many large cities, there is a high correlation between status and the allocation of space. Neighborhoods are still clearly differentiated by status as they were during the time when European, Asian, and African residential zones were clearly marked, only now African residence is less restricted. In many city council and government housing estates rents for all the units are the same, while in the others the range is often very limited. Although this pattern is probably not surprising to people familiar with western cities, it should be pointed out that in many cities in the Third World, such rigid separation on status lines is uncommon. In areas where planning and government control of neighborhoods are less prominent than in Nairobi, single areas often house people with a wider range of social statuses. One community may contain landlords, merchants, workers, and newcomers, and the available housing will be less uniform with respect to size and comfort. In such cities, ethnicity or rural birthplace may be more important than income in predicting where an individual is likely to live.

In Nairobi, rent in low-income housing estates, such as Shauri Moyo, Bahati, or Mbotela is Shs. 39/- a month. In these areas, as well as several others in the city, including two built by East African Railways for their employees, small single rooms are rented individually, and quarters for a family with children are extremely cramped. A second group of housing estates in Eastlands is more expensive but also provides some units with more than one room. Ziwani and Kaloleni, both built in the 1940s, were the first estates in Nairobi constructed with the idea of housing families rather than just working men. Rents in these areas range from about Shs. 45/– to 90/– depending on the unit.

Housing built around the time of independence recognized both the importance of multiroom units and the increasing ability and willingness of Africans to pay higher rents. The Ofafa estates, Jerusalem and Jericho, as well as Nairobi West and Kariokor, rent for Shs. 100/– to 240/– a unit and house individuals with better-paying jobs and higher-status positions in the city. A fourth level of government housing is found in housing estates built in recent years, such as Woodley, which have been constructed in formerly European areas in southwestern Nairobi and are available either for rent starting at Shs. 300/– to 400/– a month or through tenant purchase schemes.

For many years virtually all housing for Africans in Nairobi was built either by the government or by employers. It was assumed that individuals would not be willing or interested in home ownership in the city. This paternalistic policy is finally beginning to break down for several reasons: the new government does not have the same values concerning African residence and participation in Nairobi as the colonial regime, and, perhaps more important, the high rate of population growth in the last two decades has meant that government-built and financed housing cannot be constructed quickly enough to absorb the population increase. The government is now encouraging tenant purchase schemes, although these are open only to the most wealthy individuals.

Since the middle 1960s there has been a sharp increase in housing built and rented by Africans to accommodate the rapidly growing population. Some of this housing is located in illegal squatter settlements, such as Mathare Valley. A second source of new housing in the city consists of small houses, frequently built of wood at a low cost and rented by the room. Builders are often small businessmen or cooperatives which own the land on which the houses are built. No social services are provided, however, and the primary benefit is to the landlord who normally gets a full return on his investment in six months. Finally, and potentially most important in terms of both numbers and social policy, are site and service schemes, such as Kariobangi, where the city supplies basic services such as roads and water, and plot renters are responsible for constructing houses, which they can either occupy or rent. This last kind of scheme is particularly appealing because it requires a much lower unit cost than the traditional government-built housing estate and at the same time mobilizes local resources toward important social needs.

Although we are not yet sure what the effects of these changes will be, at present it can be asserted without too much qualification that spatial differentiation in Nairobi is a function of social status, and of wealth in particular, as this is the most important determinant of rents an individual is willing or able to pay. Neighborhoods are not only homogeneous by status of residents but are also related to the life-style options open to individuals. Men with lower incomes have a more difficult time supporting their wives and children in the city, but, in addition, the problem of limited space makes permanent family residence in town even more difficult. To understand the mutual interdependence of these variables, we now turn to Shauri Moyo and Kariokor, the two communities in which this study was conducted.

Two Nairobi Neighborhoods: Shauri Moyo and Kariokor
Both Shauri Moyo and Kariokor are housing estates only a few miles from the center of Nairobi, owned and maintained by the Nairobi City Council. Both are populated exclusively by Africans. Both are ethnically heterogeneous and have approximately the same proportion of residents from each of the major tribal groups.[29]

The two neighborhoods are very different, however, in most other ways. Shauri Moyo consists of 170 concrete block and corrugated iron houses, with four or six single rooms in each house, and a total of 970 rooms, which rent for Shs. 39/– each per month (Figure 1). The rooms are thirty years old and in excellent condition; however, they are small and primitive. Water is supplied to a series of service points within the estate, and people must carry it into their houses in buckets (Figure 2). Latrines and showers are communal. A small number of residents have electricity in their rooms, but few are interested in undertaking the additional cost; paraffin lanterns and flashlights are the sources of light in the evenings. Food is cooked over charcoal.

Figure 1. Shauri Moyo has 170 small cement block buildings with six single rooms and a small cooking area. Each room is rented as a separate unit.

Figure 2. Outside the houses in Shauri Moyo there are central water points and communal latrines.

In the middle of the estate there are about twenty-five shops, which are rented for Shs. 150/– per month from the Nairobi City Council. Recently about ten newer and fancier privately owned shops have been opened; all the shops are African owned and maintained. One of the city council maintained markets with 265 stalls is located at the edge of the neighborhood. In addition, there are about forty to fifty additional traders and hawkers operating in Shauri Moyo. Some, such as the charcoal dealers, are licensed by the city council. Others, such as barbers, often just nail a mirror to a tree, place a chair next to it, and are open for business. (See Figure 3.)

There are no government schools located within the housing estate, although there are several in adjacent estates. The city council does maintain an adult education school for "women and orphans" which meets in buildings adjacent to several of the council's shops. Some of the children are unable to find places in nearby schools upon arrival in the city, or their parents cannot afford the higher fees in the regular schools (Shs. 60/– per year as opposed to the standard fee of Shs. 1/– per month in the "adult" education school). The

Figure 3. A small tea stand located at the edge of Shauri Moyo.

school meets daily, in the afternoon from 2 to 4 and in the evenings from 7 to 9, and approximately 125 people are enrolled. Each morning, except Friday, one of the rooms is used as a Koranic school for the children of Muslims. Attendance is higher on Saturday and Sunday as it appears that many of the children attend government schools during the week and Koranic School on the weekend. In addition, the council maintains a Nursery School and a Homecraft Industries Center within the estate. The latter offers women instruction in sewing, cooking, and health care; attendance is very low, in comparison with some of the other estates where the council offers a similar program, probably because the fees are very high—Shs. 7/50 per month—for Shauri Moyo.

A large number of churches meet in Shauri Moyo regularly. Two denominations, the Baptists and Seventh Day Adventists, have permanent buildings in the estate. Others either rent a hall or room from the city council or hold open air meetings. Attendance at the Saturday meetings of the Seventh Day Adventist Church is large and often the congregation fills the main meeting hall, which holds about 300 people, and spills out into the front lawn. Attendance at the Baptist Church is not as great. The Church Missionary Society (CMS) holds services every Sunday at the YMCA adjacent to the estate. In addition there are several African Independent Churches that meet regularly in Shauri Moyo. The Holy Spirit Church of East Africa has been meeting in the estate for the past fifteen years on Saturdays and Sundays. The Nomiya Luo Church has been meeting inside the city council hall since the beginning of 1967. Throughout the period during which field research was conducted the following churches also held meetings, or were reported to have held meetings, in Shauri Moyo or Kamakunji (an open field adajacent to the estate): Salvation Army, Kamba Church, God's World and Holy Ghost Church, African Church of the Holy Spirit, African Independent Pentecostal Church of Kenya, Red Cross African Church in Kenya, Sinair Church of East Africa, and African Israel Church.[30]

Kariokor Estate contains a dozen four-story apartment buildings consisting of a total of 240 three-bedroom flats, which rent for Shs. 240/– plus utilities per month (Figure 4). (The average total cost is about 300/– per month.) The Estate was opened in 1964 on the

Figure 4. Kariokor consists of four-story cement block buildings. Each apartment has four rooms plus a kitchen and bathroom.

site of the Carrier Corps camp from World War I. In addition to the flats the council also constructed a large social hall for use by the residents of Kariokor and nearby estates.

Each flat has three bedrooms, a large sitting room, a kitchen with a storage section, lavatory, and shower. Cooking with charcoal cookers is prohibited, and the residents must purchase either an electric stove or a gas burner. There are running water and electricity in each flat, some of which are decorated quite luxuriously. Many have large short-wave radios, and a few have televisions.

There are no shops, schools, or churches inside the estate, although several churches, such as the Seventh Day Adventists rent a room in the social hall to hold weekly services. A city market is immediately adjacent to the estate, which is also not far from the shops in the River Road section of the city. Children from Kariokor attend schools throughout Nairobi. Many parents enroll their children in the former European or Asian schools, where the fees are higher, because they believe the quality of instruction is also. As the formerly European and Asian schools are usually located in different parts of the city, many of the children take buses to school, although some parents drive their own cars each morning.

In recent construction of housing estates the city council has followed a policy of developing "neighborhood units," including shops, social centers, and churches in addition to living units. The social hall in Kariokor is a large all-purpose meeting room, where older children play Ping-Pong, badminton, and checkers every afternoon, where movies are shown, and where dances and church services are held on the weekends. In addition, there are a number of other small rooms. During the day there are adult literacy, homecraft, and child care classes. There is room for 150 to 200 people to watch television in the evening, a library where young people come to read periodicals and do their school work, and several other rooms that are rented by various organizations for their meetings, which are usually held on Sundays. Often six or eight different organizations meet in the hall on a single Sunday. The principal users of the hall are teenagers and women who attend classes during the day. Men over 25 do not use the hall a great deal, even to watch television. The TV audiences are almost entirely young men and teenage boys.

In contrast to the facilities of the Kariokor social hall, the facilities in Shauri Moyo are makeshift. The council currently has plans to build a hall in Shauri Moyo, but the construction has not yet begun. The Shauri Moyo hall consists of several large rooms, which were once shops and are now used for the literacy classes. The council also distributes free milk to about 300 children every noon. In addition, the recently constructed YMCA, located at the edge of the estate, provides many of the recreational and library facilities usually found in the council halls. The YMCA also offers one of the few indoor basketball courts in East Africa. The Baptist Church also maintains a number of facilities similar to that of the city council halls. There are about 100 children between the ages of 8 and 18 enrolled in their recreation clubs, which meet once a week for a sports program, crafts classes, and Bible study. Women's classes in child care, nutrition, homemaking, and literacy are held during the day; literacy classes, for about 110 people (90 percent men), meet in the evenings; and in January 1968 a program of commercial courses was begun for primary school graduates who have not been able to go on to secondary school for one reason or another. The Baptist Church also has game rooms, a small library, and a television room, and free milk is distributed to 160 to 180 children at the church every day. There is another social hall in the British and American Tobacco Company housing estate, located at the northeast end of Shauri Moyo.

Shauri Moyo and Kariokor: Social Differences: Socioeconomic Status
The most striking difference between Shauri Moyo and Kariokor is socioeconomic. Table 2.2 summarizes these distinctions between the two communities. In Kariokor the education and income levels are significantly higher than in Shauri Moyo, and a far larger proportion of the population is employed in white-collar positions. In summary, Shauri Moyo is a working-class community, while Kariokor is upper middle class.

In Shauri Moyo 70 percent had either no schooling or only a few years of primary education without having passed the Kenya Primary Education (KPE) examination; in Kariokor only 12 percent had such a low level of education. While the median level of education in Shauri Moyo is a few years of primary school, the median in Kariokor is completion of the first two years of secondary education. Ninety-five percent of the respondents in Shauri Moyo have a monthly family income of less than Shs. 500/–, while only 19 percent in Kariokor have an income as low as this. The median income in Shauri Moyo is Shs. 201/– to 301/– per month, while the median in Kariokor is Shs. 801/– to 1200/– per month. In Kariokor 64 percent are employed in professional or clerical and sales positions, while only 7 percent of Shauri Moyo have comparable white-collar posts.[31]

Life-style
FAMILY ORGANIZATION AND STRUCTURE
The adult male/female ratio in both Shauri Moyo (2.1) and Kariokor (1.8) is high, as is shown in Table 2.3. Over 60 percent of the adults in each estate are male. However, the structure of households in each is very different. In Kariokor only 21 percent of the wives of married men are not residing in the city at present, while in Shauri Moyo 67 percent are outside Nairobi. The inequality of the adult male/female ratio in Kariokor occurs because there are

Table 2.2. Education, Income, and Occupation by Neighborhood

Education	Total Sample	Shauri Moyo	Kariokor
(1) No Schooling	18%	30%	2%
(2) Some Primary Education	27	40	10
(3) Primary Certificate Holder	25	23	27
(4) Form II	9	3	17
(5) Form IV	18	3	35
(6) Higher School Certificate or More	4	0	8
	101%*	99%*	99%*
Sample Size	492	270	222
Mean	2.9	2.1	4.0
Median	3	2	4
Income (Shs.)			
(1) 0 to 200/per Month	26%	43%	6%
(2) 201/to 300/per Month	19	30	4
(3) 301/to 500/per Month	16	22	9
(4) 501/to 800/per Month	12	4	22
(5) 801/to 1200/per Month	13	0	30
(6) 1201/to 2000/per Month	10	0	23
(7) Over 2000/	3	0	6
	99%*	99%*	100%
Sample Size	484	271	213
Mean	3.0	1.9	4.6
Median	3	2	5
Occupation			
Housewife	15%	16%	13%
Clerical/Sales Employee	22	6	41
Small Merchant/Artisan/Self-employed	7	10	4
Professional/Business Proprietor/ Teacher/Higher Government Official	11	1	23
Skilled Worker	14	18	8
Manual/Unskilled/Domestic Worker	20	34	3
Student	4	3	6
Farmer	1	2	0
Unemployed	7	10	3
	101%*	100%	101%*
Sample Size	495	273	222

* Column totals do not total 100 due to rounding.

Table 2.3. Sex Structure of Households by Community

	Total Sample	Shauri Moyo	Kariokor
Male	66% (330)*	68% (186)*	64% (144)*
Female	34 (168)	32 (88)	36 (80)
	100% (498)	100% (274)	100% (224)
Male/Female Ratio	1.95:1	2.1:1	1.8:1
Wife Residing in Nairobi	50% (114)	33% (47)	79% (67)
Wife Residing outside Nairobi	50 (113)	67 (95)	21 (18)
	100% (227)	100% (142)	100% (85)

* Sample sizes in parentheses.

a large number of "extra" males, typically young, unmarried, and recently arrived in the city. In Shauri Moyo the high male/female ratio is due to the low percentage of men living with their wives in the city. The adult population of Shauri Moyo is significantly older than the adults in Kariokor. The mean age in Shauri Moyo is 33.3, while it is only 26.6 in Kariokor.

Women in Kariokor have entered the labor force to a much greater extent than women in Shauri Moyo. In addition, most of those in Kariokor who are working are engaged in white-collar or professional positions, whereas the typical working woman in Shauri Moyo has a manual, unskilled, or domestic job. Of the female respondents in Kariokor, 63 percent are engaged in cash employment, while only 33 percent from Shauri Moyo are. The same relationship exists when men respondents were asked about their wives' occupation, where 41 percent of the wives of Kariokor men are employed, while only 9 percent of wives of men in Shauri Moyo are working.[32]

CONTACT WITH THE RURAL AREAS AND SOCIAL NETWORKS

There is a significant difference between Kariokor and Shauri Moyo on a variety of measures of intensity of contact with the rural areas. Kariokor, the community with the higer-status residents who are clearly more capable of existing independently in the city, also shows a higher level of contact with the rural areas than Shauri Moyo. There is greater visiting in both directions, more sending money home to rural relatives, and a greater likelihood of receiving food *from* rural relatives for Kariokor residents. In addition, they are more likely to own larger plots of land outside the city, although there is no difference in landholding per se.[33]

Residents of Shauri Moyo show a greater tendency to choose their closest friends from their own estate, birthplace, and tribe than do Kariokor residents. At the same time Shauri Moyo residents have greater urban experience in terms of the absolute number of years or the proportion of one's life in the city.[34] Urban experience therefore does not necessarily lead to the development of wide social contacts and participation in more diverse social networks.[35] In terms of both contact with the rural areas and the range of friendships in the city, Kariokor residents have more extensive and diverse social ties, whereas the Shauri Moyo residents are more likely to have ties more limited to their neighborhood or ethnic group.

Conclusions

Ethnicity, life-style, and social class are important principles of social differentiation in Nairobi and its neighborhoods. They are good predictors of an individual's social experiences and contacts in the city. Later we will examine their utility in explaining patterns of political participation and alienation. But first the ways in which ethnicity, life-style, and status operate in the context of Nairobi need to be spelled out more carefully so that their importance in politics can be clearly understood.

Chapter 3   Social Status and Life-styles in Nairobi

Urban growth in Kenya is both very rapid and very recent. Its recency is important because there are few precedents for individuals to call on in making the basic social choices that confront them in Nairobi. A man not only has some choice about where he will live in the city, but, in addition, he must decide whether his family will stay with him permanently or just visit occasionally, where his children will go to school, how he will react to requests for assistance from rural relatives, whether he will have his close friends from his own neighborhood in the city, drawn from people he knew before moving to Nairobi, or whether his friendships will be more urban based. Some of these choices, of course, are more open to some than others, as economic necessity, housing availability, and language skills impose important limitations. Likewise, many choices are not conscious; for example, most individuals hardly sit down and decide what kinds of friends they will have.

By considering how individuals respond to the city and how they make these different choices, we can learn about the values associated with living in Nairobi. In this and the next chapter, the three dimensions of urban social differentiation—social status, life-style, and ethnicity—are outlined in the context of Nairobi, and the measures of each are used in the succeeding chapters to test propositions relating social structure to political participation and alienation.

The concept of life-style is used to describe three areas of social choice facing a resident of Nairobi:[1] (1) the organization and structure of the family as a social and economic unit, (2) the strength of ties an individual in the city maintains with the rural areas, and (3) the nature of the social networks and the range of urban experiences in which individuals involve themselves.[2] According to his choices in each area, an individual can be classified as more oriented to city or rural life. In some situations, individuals are oriented toward the city out of choice, in the sense that they have the resources that would permit them to live in the city and at the same time maintain a high level of contact with the rural areas. In other cases, they are highly oriented to the city out of necessity. They may have no land outside Nairobi, their family may be dispersed, and they may not be able to afford the cost of traveling back and forth between the city and the country on a regular basis. The extent to which life-style differences are explained by social status is important because it reveals the extent to which a persons's way of life in Nairobi is dependent upon his formal schooling and his income.

Family Organization and Structure

The most significant choices a married man makes (or has made for him due to economic or social circumstances) when he moves to Nairobi concern his family. Will his wife come to live with him in the city, or will she maintain the family homestead in the rural areas? What about his children? A man does not necessarily make the same decision for each child. Should the younger ones stay with their mother wherever she lives, or is there a relative with whom the child can stay? What about the older ones? The schools are better in the city, and it is easier to get a place, especially at the secondary-school level. But food costs so much more and the limited housing accommodations will be even more crowded. Also there are the "evil" influences of the city, especially for females. Who wants to marry a woman who has been living in the town while still unmarried? Surely she must be a prostitute.

Some men bring their families to the city because they have no land in the rural areas and no relatives want to keep them on as semipermanent "boarders." Others leave their families at home because they are boarders in the city and have no place for dependents. They may share a single room with one or two other men, and their wives and/or children visit them for a short time each year. But even when a man has a room or a flat of his own, the space is often too small or the cost too large to permit his family to reside in the city on a full-time basis.

The life-style of such people is neither urban nor familial, in the manner that each is characterized by Wirth or Shevky and Bell. They certainly have not made the series of choices that Wirth suggests are characteristic of the urban way of life. On the other hand, it is equally as accurate to maintain that they do not fit the familial pattern either. They are not especially oriented to the neighborhood in which they reside, nor do they view it as a habitat that is in any way permanent.

Their "home" is not in the city, and they regard their residence there as nonpermanent, although in most cases this means at least ten to twenty years, providing that employment opportunities are available.

This "migratory" life-style will probably begin to decrease in importance with increasing industrialization and urbanization in Kenya. Individuals will not necessarily break their connections with the rural areas, but their are indications that they are beginning to move their families into Nairobi as soon as this is economically feasible. Among married men in the sample there is a positive correlation between both education (.29, $N = 224$), and income (.28, $N = 226$) and a man's wife residing in Nairobi. Men with higher education and higher income bring their wives to live with them in the city. This does not mean, however, that these people are more willing to make the city their *permanent* residence than those with lower education and income.[3]

There seem to be strong cross-pressures working in both directions. Unlike the immigrant to American cities at the turn of the century, the migrant to Nairobi both wants to return to the area from which he migrated and finds that it is economically possible to do so with relatively little strain.[4] The home area of over 90 percent of the African population of Nairobi is less than 250 miles from the city. A man can travel by bus from Nairobi to almost anywhere in Central Province for under Shs. 10/= ($1.40), while a trip from Nairobi to Kisumu is less than Shs. 20/= ($2.80). In addition, upon arrival at home a man can relax with his family and clan (until they begin to pester him for money, assuming that he is earning a great deal in the city).

WOMEN IN THE CITY

If a man's wife resides with him in Nairobi, a choice must be made about how the wife will use her time. One of the major objections that Kenyan men have to their wives living in the city is that "there is nothing for them to do." A woman with only minimal education can either be a housewife, an unskilled worker, or a trader, but both capital and experience are necessary to start a business. Nairobi men are just beginning to accept the idea that it is reasonable for a woman to be a housewife rather than engage in a role that is more productive economically. At the same time, more women are attending school and learning the skills as secretaries or teachers that ensure them employment in the city if they desire it.

In western societies the dichotomy between career women and family women is more meaningful than in Kenya. The traditional system of child care in all of the major tribes is such that the mother delegates a great deal of the responsibility to others, especially the older children. This permits the mother to spend the entire day engaging in economic activities such as planting and sowing the crops or trading in the markets.[5] The pattern in the city has not been to assign full-time responsibility to the older children to permit the mother to work, since one reason women work is to pay for the school fees for the children. Instead women often employ teenage girls, who in most cases are hired through family ties with the rural areas, to serve as *ayahs* (baby-sitters and maids). The girls, for the most part, are uneducated and come from poorer families and welcome the opportunity to work and to come to the city. A woman with the skills and the desire to work in Nairobi is not constrained by the size of her family. Working women, who cannot afford the cost of an *ayah*,[6] take advantage of the day nurseries the city maintains as well as of certain informal communal child care arrangements. Several women, who live in close proximity to one other and who have children of similar age, will often take turns caring for one another's children.

THE MEANING OF THE CITY FOR MEN AND WOMEN

Within Kenya tribal society, urban life has a very different meaning for men and women.[7] It is perfectly reasonable for a young man to move to the city after finishing his education to earn money so he can marry. Once he starts his family it is also understandable if he says he must remain in Nairobi to earn money to educate and feed his children, to purchase more land, or to obtain capital to allow him to plant cash crops such as tea or coffee. A single woman, however, who announces that she wants to come to the city to work, even in such white-collar positions as a secretary or teacher, upsets her relatives. They warn her that she will be considered a prostitute and will have a difficult time ever finding a husband. If the woman is already married and she moves to the town to join her husband, the family in the rural areas may be displeased for other reasons. First of all, they will not understand what she will do in the town that might be as economically productive as her work on the farm at home. Second, they expect both the woman and man to remain on the land of the husband's family. They can understand his leaving the land, however, because of economic necessity, but this is not true for the wife. Third, she is an integral part of the homestead in the rural areas, and there are certain chores and responsibilities assigned to her which someone else must assume if she leaves. Last, they are worried about having the children raised in the city. There is the fear of the unknown and complex as well as the more specific feeling that the children will grow up not knowing their tribal customs and maybe even marrying someone of a different tribe if they are raised in the town.

A great deal of the present negative feeling toward women in the city exists because many of the women who lived in Nairobi in earlier decades were social outcasts in rural society and earned their living in Nairobi by prostitution or illicit beer brewing. After a period some accumulated a bit of capital and built houses, in which they rented rooms to other prostitutes or to single men or started businesses. Gatheru describes these women:

There were, however, a large number of African women who had left their husbands in the rural area because of various matrimonial causes, such as barrenness, adultery, their husbands' polygamy or unfaithfulness with loose women in the city while they themselves were working hard in the Reserves, infidelity to which they felt forced to retaliate.

These women were working in the city as 'ayahs'—taking care or children or baby-sitting for the Europeans generally and for some Asians. One might call many of them prostitutes. As a result men in the city could call upon them and invite them to a dance or evening out. Some of these women were wealthy and, in fact, wealthier than many men in the city and they owned some mud-built houses in one of the African locations called Majengo (Pumwani).[8]

The feeling that single women in the city still fit into this category is widespread in the rural areas of Kenya. One moves to the city from necessity. A man goes to make money; a woman goes if she no longer fits into the social structure of rural society. For a young, unattached female to move to the city because she "wants to live there" is a great mistake in the eyes of her rural family.

Contact with the Rural Areas
Residents of Nairobi maintain a high degree of contact with their families in the rural areas of the country. The city is not home, and even young people express a desire to live elsewhere if possible. In one of the pretests of the interview schedule, each respondent was asked if he or she would like to live in another part of the country or in Nairobi for the next five years. The sample was young (the average age was 26.5 years) and yet only 54 percent ($N = 98$) said they wanted to stay in Nairobi. When they were asked where they would prefer to live when they are old, only 23 percent ($N = 97$) chose the city.

Nairobians do not see any necessity to commit themselves psychologically to an urban life. They are able to live in the city for years while at the same time maintaining the belief that it is not their home. The high level of interaction between the city and rural areas reinforces this outlook, so that if one asks residents of the city, "Where is your home?" very few name a location in Nairobi.

At first glance, it would appear that the maintenance of these ties would serve to ease the transition from rural to urban life. Individuals do not close all the doors behind them, as they leave open the possibility of returning to the rural areas at any time. An alternative hypothesis is that the maintenance of the strong ties serves to subject individuals to severe cross-pressures. They must respond to demands, often quite contradictory, from the rural and urban environments in which they exist. The rural norm is to aid any relative in need. If a relative from the rural areas appears in the city, therefore, he should be housed, clothed, and fed until he can support himself. However, in the city, there is not a great deal of space, and the only way to obtain food is by spending cash. Men in the city find that they must set limits to the amount of aid they can give to relatives; in fact there are pressures toward disengagement from the rural family in order to enjoy the fruits of one's own urban labor. The following is typical of the pressures created by rural relatives:

A secondary school student who had spent his whole life in Nairobi, managed to get a job during his school holiday working for the government during the voter registration campaign in August 1967. He was living in the rural areas with his family and managed to save almost the entire salary and had Shs. 200/= which he was going to bring back to the city to be spent during the school year. Just before returning to Nairobi three relatives approached him and presented him with a list of things they needed. He bought almost everything on the list and when he arrived in the city his monies were almost exhausted. He said that he couldn't refuse their request because they would think badly of him. He said he couldn't really tell whether they really needed everything on the list, but he just had to accept their word.[9]

INTENSITY OF URBAN-RURAL CONTACT

Each respondent in the two estates was asked a series of questions to determine the intensity of contact he or she maintains with the rural areas. The questions concerned four areas of activity: visiting and spending time at home, having relatives visit and spend time in the city, receiving food from the rural areas, and sending money home to support individuals living in the rural areas. In addition, each person was asked whether or not he owned land outside the city.[10]

Table 3.1 shows that the level of contact between the individuals living in the city and their rural homes is quite high. Four-fifths of the sample indicated that they had engaged in three of the four behaviors, at least at the minimum level. Seventy-nine percent reported that they had spent time with their families in the rural areas in the past year; 80 percent reported that at least one relative came into Nairobi and visited during the past year; 81 percent reported that they sent money to help relatives at home at least once in the past year. Half reported receiving food from their families in the rural areas during the past year. In addition, 59 percent owned some land outside the city.

Landownership, or at least land rights, is often crucial to the maintenance of ties between an individual in the city and his relatives in the rural areas. Often the landholding is small. Only 20 percent of the sample have farms of seven acres or more, while 24 percent have farms of less than three acres in size. The land is hardly adequate to allow a man to support his wife and children without the added burden of paying taxes and school fees. On the other hand, a man

Table 3.1. Intensity of Contact with the Rural Areas

1. In the past year what period of time have you spent with your family at home?

None	22%	($N = 109$)
One week or less	16	(81)
One week to month	32	(157)
1–3 months	15	(73)
3–6 months	6	(31)
Over 6 months	9	(46)
	100%	(497)

2. How often did you travel home this past year?

Never	22%	(109)
Once	29	(141)
Several times	34	(167)
Once a month	8	(41)
Once a week or more	7	(34)
	100%	(492)

3. Have relatives from home come into Nairobi and visited you in the past year?

Yes	81%	(402)
No	19%	(94)
	100%	(496)

4. About how many people came to visit you?

0	20%	(94)
1–5	53	(257)
6–10	13	(65)
11–20	4	(21)
Over 20	10	(46)
	100%	(483)

5. Many families sent food to their relatives living in Nairobi. In the past year has your family at home sent you any food?

Yes	49%	(244)
No	51	(252)
	100%	(496)

6. (IF YES) How often did they send you food?

Once a week or more	3%	(16)
About once a month	7	(34)
Several times during the year	34	(168)
Once	8	(38)
Never	49	(244)
	101%*	(498)

7. In the past year have you sent any money to help relatives at home?

Yes	81%	(399)
No	19	(97)
	100%	(494)

8. (IF YES) How often did you send money?

Once a month	44%	(218)

Table 3.1. (continued)

A few times this year	31	(151)
Once this year	6	(28)
Never	19	(97)
	100%	(494)

9. Do you have a *shamba* (land) outside of Nairobi?

Yes	59%	(294)
No	41	(203)
	100%	(497)

10. (IF YES) How many acres is it?

No farm	41%	(203)
1–3 acres	24	(117)
4–6 acres	15	(74)
7–10 acres	9	(47)
10–20 acres	6	(31)
Over 20 acres	5	(24)
	100%	(496)

* Column percentages do not add up to 100 due to rounding.

with a small holding and several children will often leave his wife home to cultivate the land, while he moves to the city to earn a cash income. When a man moves to the city with his wife and family, he has two alternatives with regard to the utilization of his land. He may ask one of his relatives—often a brother—to maintain the land, sometimes allowing the brother to till the land as if it were his own, until the man or his wife returns from the city. The other alternative is to send his wife, and the younger children (that is, those not yet in school) home to the rural areas for several months a year to maintain the farm. This choice may mean sending the wife home at the beginning of the planting season to do all the work herself and to return to the city only when the crops have been harvested and marketed. Or it may mean that the wife will travel home for several weeks at the beginning of the planting season, hire several people to work on the farm, and then return to the city until it is almost time to harvest the crops, when she or her husband will again visit the farm, make the necessary arrangements for harvesting and marketing, and then return to the city again.

CONTACT WITH THE RURAL AREAS AND SOCIOECONOMIC STATUS

The intensity of an individual's contact with the rural areas is a func-

Table 3.2. Contact with the Rural Areas by Education, Income, Landownership, Length of Residence in Nairobi in Years, Percentage of Life Spent in Nairobi, and Cinema Attendance in Past Year[11]

	Correlation	Sample Size
Education	.20*	(492)
Income	.29*	(484)
Land owner	.19*	(497)
Size of Landholding	.18*	(494)
Length of Residence	−.16*	(496)
Percentage of Life in City	−.15*	(496)
Cinema Attendance	.19*	(494)

* Significant at the .01 level.

tion of socioeconomic status. The higher the socioeconomic status of an individual, the greater the intensity of his contact with rural areas. People who have the skills most essential for survival in the urban community are the individuals for whom the rural ties are maintained most intensely. Thus, individuals do not sever their ties with their families in the rural areas as soon as they acquire the necessary skills and move into the urban economy. Rather, urban success promotes a strengthening of ties to the countryside.

The index measuring the intensity of an individual's contact with the rural area is correlated with a number of socioeconomic indicators, as is shown in Table 3.2. The data indicate that the intensity of contact with the rural areas is higher, the greater an individual's education and income, the larger his land holding, the shorter his length of residence in the city in years or the smaller the percentage of his life that he had spent living in Nairobi, and if he had attended a cinema in the city center in the past year. Urban-based resources thus assist a person in maintaining rural ties and a status in the rural setting.

The pattern is similar to the one found by Clignet and Sween in a study of polygyny in the Ivory Coast. They report that among men the incidence of polygyny decreases with increasing education, income, and length of residence until the highest levels of each of these indicators. At this point, the incidence of polygyny again rises. Their explanation is what they call the "modernization of means rather than ends."[12] A low-level clerk with a primary school plus education is unable to take a second wife simply because he has neither the resources to secure her, nor the ability to support her after the marriage. Such persons, they argue, are monogamous not out of social choice but because their economic condition leaves them with no alternative to monogamy. Individuals higher up the socioeconomic status ladder are able to arrange and afford plural marriages, which they do.

In Nairobi, individuals who sever their ties with the rural areas, or maintain them at a low intensity, appear to do so because of economic necessity rather than because of a social choice. The data suggest that, given greater resources, the level of contact would be higher. For a man to travel home frequently, to send money home regularly, or to support relatives in the city, he must have a regular job paying a decent salary. Individuals with a higher income, with greater education, and with larger landholdings in the rural areas are more likely to be in an economic position to maintain these ties at a high level.

Social Networks in Nairobi[13]
Individuals in a city locate themselves in social as well as geographical space. When a person first arrives in Nairobi, he stays with relatives from the rural areas. Eighty-five percent of the sample ($N = 100$) in one pretest of the interview schedule reported staying with a relative when they first arrived in Nairobi. After acquiring a job the newcomer is expected to move into a place of his own or at least to assume a proportionate share of the household expenses. Even when an individual decides to obtain a room or flat in Nairobi, his choice is greatly limited by a lack of available housing. The city council of Nairobi, the largest renter in the city, claims that there is a waiting list for council housing which is larger than the 15,000 flats the council maintains. To some extent a man will take anything he can get in the Eastlands section of town. If he has an opportunity to obtain a flat that costs more than he is able to pay, he will often find one or two people, to share it with him, rather than pass up the opportunity to acquire housing. Another consequence of the great shortage of housing is that there is little choice exercised with regard to preferred neighborhoods of residence. If a man is asked, "Where is a good place for you to live in Nairobi?" his reply is likely to be, "Wherever

I can find a room." The last significant aspect of the housing situation
is that there is not a great deal of housing owned by Africans in the
city. Small areas of the city are not residentially segregated by clans or
large extended families, in the way they are in many West African
cities.

In Nairobi there are few areas in which there is a highly developed
sense of community or neighborhood. Not only do individuals generally have minimal commitment to the city, as discussed earlier,
but, in addition, their ties to their urban neighborhoods are also weak
because such a great proportion of their social and economic activities occurs outside them. Despite the efforts of the city council in
recent years to make each of their housing estates into "meaningful
neighborhood units," by building shops, social centers, and churches
in addition to living units, the neighborhood of residence is often not
more than a place to sleep, especially for adult men. Individuals continually travel to other estates to visit friends or relatives. In any
group of men relaxing in a bar or a flat on Saturday or Sunday afternoon, chances are that only a few will live in the estate where the bar
or flat is located.

Teenage boys and, to a lesser extent, women take advantage of the
facilities offered in the social halls. Women sit outside with their children during the day, talking together and helping each other with
their household tasks. When asked in which estate their three closest
friends lived,[14] women indicated a significantly higher percentage of
close friends in their own estates than men.[15] For the entire sample,
only 22 percent of their closest friends lived in the respondent's own
estate; and 87 percent reported that they had either none or only
one of their three best friends in their own estate.

Individuals' social networks are determined by ethnicity and social
class more than by neighborhood. Other criteria such as common
place of employment, religion, or age are also important. The proportion of most church congregations living in the estate in which the
church is located is not high. Individuals attend a church depending
upon, first, which mission operated in their home areas, and, second,
where their friends or relatives in Nairobi attend church. Thus, the
congregations of most churches are drawn from a large number of the

neighborhoods in the city. Only 6 percent of the respondents in the
sample drawn from Kariokor and Shauri Moyo reported attending
church in their estates. ($N = 437$) The remainder, and great majority,
travel to churches in different parts of the city. In some of the churches
that hold services several times a week, particularly the African Independent Churches, religious interest also provides the basis for
most social interaction.

The selection of friends in Nairobi is limited by an individual's
language skills. A person with minimal education and recently arrived
in the city is only articulate and at ease in his vernacular, although
he may have some knowledge of Swahili. Swahili and English, the two
nontribal languages of widespread use in the city, are the first languages for only a small proportion of the African population. They
are used in the fulfillment of specific tasks, such as government business, which is mainly conducted in English, or petty trade, which usually goes on in Swahili; but a person is not necessarily competent
enough to use them in other areas of life. As a consequence of the mul-
tilingual situation, people are limited in the number of persons
with whom they can develop close friendships and feel at ease. This is
reflected in the fact that 83 percent of the respondents reported that
their closest friend was from their own tribe.[16]

The City and Thresholds in the Social Life Cycle
Very few adults living in Nairobi were born in the city. Only 20 of
the 498, or 4 percent, of the adults in the sample in Shauri Moyo and
Kariokor were born in the city. The average length of residence in the
city is 9.6 years, and the average proportion of life spent in the city
is 29 percent. Census data show that the age structure of the Nairobi
population is more clustered around the 20 to 40 age groups than the
population of the country as a whole.

Kenyans do not consider Nairobi a desirable place to celebrate
major thresholds in the social life cycle: birth, initiation, marriage,
and death. While initiation ceremonies, such as circumcision rituals,
are performed within the city, there is a definite preference to hold
them in the rural areas whenever possible. In part this feeling is due
to the greater control that the police exert over city residents; in part

it is due to a certain degree of self-consciousness concerning traditional
ceremonies and rituals in tribally mixed areas of the city (the areas
in the city in which the author is aware that Kikuyu circumcision ceremonies are conducted all are areas in which the Kikuyu population is overwhelmingly in the majority); and in part it is due to the
desire to conduct them on one's own land.

The same attitude is true for marriage and death. Most marriages
take place outside the city. Data from one of the pretests showed that
85 percent of the married individuals in the sample reported being
married outside Nairobi. A related aspect is the low proportion of
intertribal marriages; marriages taking place in the rural areas are
almost invariably intratribal. In the present sample about 10 percent
of the married individuals reported that their spouse was not from
their tribe (35 out of 346).

Nairobi is not a "good" place to get married, partially because
Nairobi is not a "good" place to find a wife. The older generation
suspects that a single woman living in the city is by definition a prostitute. Men, on the other hand, are reluctant to marry women they
meet in the city because they are often afraid that the women will be
too independent and uncontrollable. They realize that a woman who
has lived in the city for several years may not look kindly on the idea
of living alone with her children on her husband's small plot of land
while he stays in the city. When young, unmarried men in the city are
asked if they would prefer to marry a woman from the city or one
from the rural areas, they invariably choose a woman from the country.

Nairobi is not the place a man wants to die. Most individuals make
plans to leave the city after their productive years are passed, or as
soon as it is no longer possible to find employment. This is reflected
in the figures already cited showing the high level of contact with the
rural areas. Only 3 percent of the adults in Kariokor and Shauri Moyo
are over the age of 50; and only 16 percent are over 40. Burial societies,
on the scale which some authors describe in West African cities, are
not found in Nairobi. There are available some forms of burial insurance, which pay the cost of sending the boy of the deceased to the
rural areas in the case of death. Much more prominent, however, is a
spontaneous collection taken by relatives and close friends when a
death occurs unexpectedly in Nairobi.

LAND AND SECURITY

Thus far, Kenyans for the most part have shown reluctance to commit themselves permanently to urban life. Money is usually invested in land in the rural areas before it will be spent on a house or business in the city. This is explained as "security." It is expressed in terms of a "low-risk" strategy. Men argue that if they die, their wives can quickly spend cash that is left or lose a business through mismanagement, but they can always live on the *shamba* (farm) and plant enough to support the children. "If the political climate changes," they argue; "if I lose my job"; "if we have bad times here again. . . ." In each of these cases, land is more important than a house or business in the city, because with land, even a small holding, an individual can manage the minimal act of survival, if not prosperity.

One important constraint and/or alternative to the purchase of land for men working in the city is the burden placed upon them to pay school fees for their children. These days, at least among the major agricultural tribes of the country—the Kikuyu, Kamba, Baluhya, and Luo—there is a great pressure for education. Children want to attend school and parents want to send them. Within the city of Nairobi, the City Education Department asserts that there is a space in school for every child who presents himself with the fees. In other parts of the country, this is not as true. Education is often viewed as the same sort of investment in the future as land. A man who is able to see his son obtain a Secondary School Certificate or higher degree knows that the child will assume some (if not most) of the responsibility for the education of his younger siblings, as well as take care of his parents as they grow older. This may mean, for example, that a father deliberately forgoes the purchase of land in order to educate his son, hoping that once his son has obtained a higher degree he will purchase the land on which his parents will reside.

The old people in the city are the least educated, and they realize the limitations this creates. There are many men and women who migrated to the city twenty and thirty years ago, obtained employment, and have remained in the city. Many are now being displaced either because of the changes in employment opportunities in recent years or because the educational system is now turning out a large number of graduates who can often do the job better than the older, less-educated employees. In the first category one can find a number of Africans now seeking employment who had previously worked as domestic servants "in the days when every European had four or five Africans working for him." In the second are the Africans who were trained as petty clerks, who are being replaced by younger people who can assume greater responsibility on the job because of their more complete educational training. Most of these men with clerk's training are still in their productive years and have families to support either in the rural areas or Nairobi; they remain in the city, hanging on to a job if they have one, desperately looking if they don't. But time is not on their side. Each year an increasing number of secondary-school graduates come to the city to find employment, and each year for the past several years jobs are becoming harder and harder to come by for men with more limited skills. But if they can just manage to put at least one son through secondary school, then he will get a good paying job, and then he can buy land or coffee trees for his father who worked so hard to educate him, or so they believe.

Social Status and Life-style

The concept of life-style shows the orientations that people have toward living in the city and the social choices that are made as a result of this cluster of attitudes. Life-style choices, at least in Nairobi at the present time, are not made independently of social status considerations. Whether or not a man's family is residing with him in the city, the level of contact he maintains with the rural areas, his length of residence in the city, and his friendship choices are all functions of

Table 3.3. Summary of Correlations between Life-style Indicators and Social Status

	Education	Income
Where Wife Is Residing	−.29 (224)	−.28 (225)
Contact with the Rural Areas Index	.20* (492)	.28* (484)
Percent of Close Friends from Estate	−.19* (470)	−.10† (461)
Percent of Close Friends from Birthplace	−.22* (457)	−.21* (458)
Percent of Close Friends from City	.04 (472)	.08 (463)
Length of Residence in Nairobi in Years	−.36* (490)	−.19* (482)

* Significant at the .01 level.
† Significant at the .05 level.
Sample sizes in parentheses.

his level of income and education as is shown in Table 3.3. Life-style choices, then, are at least in part socioeconomic in origin.[17] At the same time, the correlations between the measures of the two dimensions are not particularly high, indicating that there is a good deal of variation in life-style choices which is unrelated to status. Before discussing the effect of life-style and status on political participation and alienation, we now turn to a consideration of urban ethnicity in Nairobi.

Chapter 4   Ethnicity as an Enduring Factor in Urban Politics

The question of relations between ethnic groups in urban areas is visible in every large city in the world where there are distinct cultural groups. These groups are important because of their visibility and the relative ease with which they can be mobilized in social and political conflicts. This chapter explores several hypotheses concerning the strength of ethnic identification and ethnic ties in Nairobi, and the following chapters consider the significance of ethnicity in explaining patterns of political participation and alienation.

There are two general approaches to the study of ethnicity in urban areas. The first views ethnicity as a manifestation of certain cultural forms, while the second is more concerned with it as a form of identification and as a basis of social action. The first approach sees the urban environment as one in which cultural assimilation and detribalization occur, and the second tends to focus upon the differences between groups that persist in the urban environment.

Each approach tries to explain different sets of behavior. The first concentrates on manifest actions associated with "ethnic" behavior throughout the world: modes of dress, religion and ritual practices, special foods, and often a distinct language. The immigrant, and even more frequently his children, often abandons, and usually modifies all of these the longer he stays in the new city. The second approach sees ethnicity as one basis of social organization; it is the strength of the ethnic identification and not any particular cultural marker of ethnicity, that mobilizes people to act as corporate groups for social and political purposes.[1]

Many have assumed for too long that a decrease in ethnic behavior in the cultural sphere is automatically related to the diminishing importance of ethnicity as the basis for social and political organization. Evidence in the United States is that even after several generations ethnicity is still a crucial factor in urban politics.[2] In Africa where individuals are often living only a small distance from the center of their group's territory, and where there is an even shorter history of large-scale interaction between groups, it cannot be assumed that ethnicity will be any less important.

In this chapter we shall first discuss two approaches which assume that changes in the cultural sphere will be related to changes in the social and political one, and then present the "cultural pluralism" perspective that avoids making this assumption. The second section presents data to show that in Nairobi ethnic identification persists despite cultural changes.

In studying ethnicity or tribalism in Africa a necessary initial distinction is between tribal structure and tribal identification.[3] Much of the early literature on African cities focused upon the process of "detribalization." Individuals who left their home areas for the town removed themselves from the local chiefly authority and from the day-to-day social sanctions that could be invoked in the tribal society.[4] "The one is a system of social relationships, the other is a category of interaction within a wider system," is the way that Mitchell distinguishes between the two.[5] In the urban areas, ethnicity can be defined as identification that provides a basis (but not the only one) for social organization. In the cities, many institutions develop on a tribal basis. In West Africa, voluntary associations are more prominent than they have been thus far in East Africa.[6] However, in Nairobi the number of tribally based welfare associations is growing quickly. Another Nairobi institution with tribal roots is the African independent church. Today in Nairobi there are at least 46 such congregations,[7] many of which hold regular services in the vernacular and whose membership comes almost entirely from one ethnic group (and often from one location in the rural areas). Even the European-based churches often have a tribal character because the city's residents tend to attend the church that had missions in their home areas. In Nairobi the Friends are predominantly Abaluhya, the Presbyterians are Kikuyu, and those who attend the African Inland Mission Church mainly Kamba.

But even with the creation of such institutions at the formal level, and the development of kin and ethnic friendship networks at the informal level, the social control that fellow tribesmen have over one another in the city is less than at home. Role differentiation has divided life into more independent spheres of activity. Economic activity, for example, becomes divorced from place of residence, and a higher percentage of interactions takes place on the basis of established regulations for highly specific purposes. None of the institutions, even

58   CHAPTER 4

including groups of tribal elders found in the city, are capable of or attempt to exert the control over individuals' lives that the tribal ties provide at home.[8] Most groups of elders, for example, involve themselves only in cases where all parties agree that they should hear the case. Otherwise individuals are advised to seek redress through the court system.

"Familiarity Breeds Understanding"
Students of African politics have adopted different "models," usually implicitly, in considering ethnicity. Studies of the politics of the independence era focused upon the growth of national parties, controlled by politicians partly trying to convince the colonial administration that they represented a territorial wide movement, and partly seeking political power for themselves. Usually these politicians were the most educated members of the society. In many cases they had studied overseas for years and had become converted to some form of Pan Africanist ideology, and hence it is not difficult to understand the hypothesis that emerged: "The greater an individual's education, the less tribal and the more national or even international his political outlook." A corollary of this proposition is that if a society is able to educate a greater proportion of its population, then tribal antagonisms will continue to grow less important.

A major source of the theoretical underpinning of this approach is the first section of Daniel Lerner's *The Passing of Traditional Society*.[9] Lerner defined modernization as a process of expanding individuals' world views, and the development of an increasing ability to empathize with situations or persons outside one's own immediate experience. He presented data showing the cumulative effect of urbanization, literacy, and media participation on political participation. Societies urbanize (and industrialize), individuals are educated, they use their education involving themselves in the mass media, and finally they participate in the political system.

The theory is not very elegant, as Lerner fails to articulate the mechanisms involved in the process. Implicit in his theorizing is the view that identification with older cultural groupings diminishes as individuals adopt western habits in the cities. He makes no mention, for example, of the growth of secondary institutions, the decline of face-to-face, personal political and social organizations, or any of the sociological tradition from Toennies and Durkheim which might have provided the necessary theoretical link. He even neglected to consider one of the major findings of the group of scholars working with him at the time who discovered the importance of "opinion leaders" at all levels of society and within all social groups.[10] Last, Lerner shows no appreciation of political institutions and participation patterns in traditional society.

Lerner does not deal directly with the problem of ethnicity. However, the perspective he adopted was admirably suited to students grappling with it in Africa. Education, increased income, and development in general would serve as the impetus that would expand empathy in each country. A nation with more empathetic individuals would be one in which there would be a greater tolerance for the views and customs of different groups. If we were to draw concentric circles on a map, representing the perceptual life space of an individual with his birthplace at the center, then as the modernization process progresses the circles would grow progressively larger. The model inherent in Lerner's theorizing would not have us stop at national boundaries, and, in fact, the rhetoric and support for Pan Africanism in the independence era seemed to confirm this model. It is now obvious that it underestimated the strength of forces that limit to a handful the number of politicians adopting such a position today. There was little appreciation of the strong rewards for being a "parochial" politician.

The basis of this argument is the erroneous assumption that contact and awareness breed understanding and cooperation. In learning theory terms it assumes that contact (stimulus), either face to face or otherwise, will always be rewarding and thus the conditioned response will be the development of positive affect between the groups. However, there are times when familiarity breeds contempt. When groups meet in situations of great resource scarcity—whether in the job market of an African city or the slums of an American one—the contact situation may be viewed as "punishing," not "rewarding."[11] Groups may come to know more about each other, and at the same time distrust and hatred may grow rather than decline.

The "Melting Pot" Approach

A second approach is drawn from the "melting pot" concept that is so prominent and overstressed in the literature on American cities.[12] It places greater stress on personal experience than does the first approach and also introduces more of a temporal element because it suggests that some of the most important changes are those which occur between, rather than within, generations. This perspective asserts that ethnicity declines because of direct exposure to new cultural forms which forces individuals to develop attitudes and behaviors different, and less ethnic, from those of their parents.

Studies in this group focus upon the diminishing importance of certain cultural forms, such as distinctive foods, modes of dress, or language, in the second and third generations. This, it is asserted, has served to assimilate individuals into their new culture. The difficulty with this view is that it insists on adopting a static conception of each ethnic group in the past. It fails to see evolution and changes in attitudes and behaviors of the group occurring across previous generations. Also, while these studies have carefully documented the ways in which immigrants or their children have acquired the new skills and shed older behaviors, they have devoted little attention to the uses to which these skills were put.

The evidence is that immigrants in both African and American cities have tended to use their newly acquired skills to strengthen their ethnically based formal associations and to continue their ethnically based friendship networks.[13] One consequence is that ethnic groups still constitute voting blocs that can be expected to deliver huge majorities to one candidate or party. Wirth's study of the Chicago ghetto early in this century shows the maintenance of ethnic associations in Chicago's Jewish community over four or five generations.[14] As successive generations of immigrants, first from Germany, and later from Eastern Europe, moved into the ghetto, the children of the previous generation, now educated and culturally assimilated, would move to a more fashionable neighborhood. The children were "culturally" American insofar as they spoke English fluently, dressed as other Americans did, and felt at ease in a much wider world than their parents did. However, Wirth carefully pointed out the newer, all-Jewish institutions they created in the new neighborhoods. The starting place was always the religious institution, the synagogue, but the religion practiced there was less orthodox than in the ghetto, and, as Gans showed in the 1950s the religious importance had clearly become second to the importance of the temple as a social center in the community.[15]

"Cultural Pluralism"

The "melting pot" approach is an assimilationist view of the contact situation between groups. It implies that out of the diversity something new and homogeneous emerges. Such an assumption is empirically wrong. What has developed in America and what seems to be developing in Africa is more along the lines of the "cultural pluralism" model. In this situation different groups coexist side by side, each with its own cultural norms and standards and having a minimum of interaction, except at specific points—often the marketplace. The American experience, with the important exception of Black–White relations, has been the development of an accommodation, a modus vivendi, where each group retains a great deal of autonomy and each respects the other's differences, while at the same time evolving more similar cultural forms. At other times, however, relations between the groups are far more hostile, such as in South Africa. Therefore, it is useful to consider the degree of pluralism in a society as a variable, rather than as an all-or-nothing matter. Van den Berghe defines a society as pluralistic:[16]

to the extent that it is structurally segmented and culturally diverse. In more operational terms, pluralism is characterized by the relative absence of value consensus; the relative rigidity and clarity of group definition, or at least, of lack of integration and complementarity between various parts of the social system; the segmentary and specific character of relationships, and the relative existence of sheer institutional duplication (as opposed to functional differentiation or specialization) between various segments of society.

Instead of assuming that interacting groups will grow more similar and less antagonistic, this approach recognizes that relations between groups may grow either more or less fluid. This is because it defines groups in subjective rather than objective terms.[17] Rather than considering ethnicity as a set of cultural characteristics that an individual either does or does not possess, a subjective definition is more

useful in the urban context. A person is considered to be a member of
a certain group if he considers himself to be a member of that group,
and if others in his community consider him a member of that group.
Gluckman describes "tribalism in towns" as "primarily a means of
classifying the multitude of Africans of heterogeneous origin who live
together in the towns, and this classification is the basis on which a
number of new African groupings such as burial and mutual help
societies are formed to meet the needs of urban life."[18] Wallerstein
distinguishes between continued attachment to tribal custom and
"tribalism without social structure," which is the "persistence of loyalties and values, which stem from a particular form of social organization."[19] Increasing urbanization means that "loyalty to the ethnic
community is coming to supersede loyalty to the tribal community
and government."[20] Van den Berghe points out the dynamic manner
in which contact between groups often strengthens ethnic identification. "Studies of culture contact have overemphasized 'borrowing'
of cultural items as the major process of change through contact. . .
the fact that cultures almost invariably *adjust to* and *react against*
as well as *borrow from* one another has, I think, been underempha-
sized."[21]

Ethnicity, as a basis for social and political action, is defined situa-
tionally. Throughout Africa fine distinctions are drawn between the
subgroups of a particular tribe within the tribe's home area, but when
members leave the home area for town these subgroup differences are
less important and individuals begin to identify themselves as part of
the larger group. In Kenya, for example, the Abaluhya are now considered to be one tribe, although the term "Abaluhya" did not come
into use until about 1945.[22] The Abaluhya have no centralized
political structure, but they share a common language and have many
similar customs across the different subgroups. Within Western
Province, many people still focus upon the between group differences;
however, in Nairobi they are far less important in comparison with
the differences between the Abaluhya and other tribes. In the city
there is an Abaluhya Union as well as other organizations that ignore
these between group differences.

In West Africa ethnicity is sometimes defined by occupation, rather
than by the more customary cultural traits. The Doula in the Ivory

Coast have traditionally served as the country's long distance traders. The name itself roughly means "trader from the north," and people from Guinea, Mali, and Upper Volta are all included in this ethnic group.

Individuals do not have the psychological need to make an extremely large number of distinctions. Seeking order in their universe, they develop a few basic categories in which to group people they meet. In Nairobi whether a man from Uganda is Batoro or Baganda is generally unimportant. To the Kenyan the salient fact is his "Ugandanness," a situation that is quite different than in Kampala. There are numerous divisions within the Indian community in East Africa, but Africans generally lump them together as *Wahindi*. Ethnicity, as a basis for social action, then, depends upon both how individuals regard themselves and how others regard them. A perceptual definition of ethnicity means that it is viewed as a series of cues which have a varying importance to different actors across a variety of situations.[23] There is usually an association between these cues and a myth of common origin or common experience which links the individuals in each group together and which outsiders also recognize.

In his study of the Xhosa in East London, Mayer found two distinctive cultural groups—the "School people" and the "Red people." The first "are products of the mission and the school, holding up Christianity, literacy and other Western ways as ideals." The latter "are the traditional Xhosa conservatives who still stand by the indigenous way of life, including the pagan Xhosa religion."[24] There is minimal contact between the two communities. Each has its own values and behavior patterns. Red migrants in town take part in an "encapsulating social network" that is an "extension of the community at home" and constitutes the most effective vehicle of opinion formation and is the guardian of morality.[25] The Red migrants have created a host of institutions designed to maintain the values of their community, while at the same time permitting the individual to participate in the modern cash economy. In East London there is no inevitable blending of the differences between the two groups. The adoption of new values in one sphere, for example, the economic, does not necessarily mean that different values must be adopted in all others. The Red migrants have created new institutions that help to preserve in a new setting their ethnic identification and behaviors in those spheres of life considered most important.

The "pluralist" model is compatible with a definition of ethnicity that is perceptual, and that allows for change, but not necessarily in only one direction over time. Glazer and Moynihan, in discussing New York's major ethnic groups, argue that ethnicity is not necessarily any less important for third or fourth generation New Yorkers than it was for their immigrant ancestors.[26] However, they argue that what changes across generations are the forms of ethnicity which serve as the basis of identification. Typically, the behaviors that change first are the most visible, such as dress and language, but what is crucial is that identification and participation in common institutions are maintained. What continues is the existence of several distinct social groups with their own norms and values and with a far higher intensity of interactions within their own group than across groups, especially in the more intimate spheres of social life.

The heterogeneity of urban social life is bound to produce culturally diverse subgroups within its population. These groups are primarily ascriptive and serve to satisfy the expressive needs of individuals. By evolving across generations they provide something meaningful in terms of contemporary life, rather than providing an individual with something his grandfather considered important. This argument should not be construed to read that there are no individuals without such group attachments or in the process of weakening their attachments.

Ethnicity is a variable, not a constant, in urban areas. It is not always the basis for social organization as Epstein, and others at the Rhodes-Livingstone Institute, have shown.[27] Epstein treated the salience of ethnicity as a variable and examined it across a range of situations. He showed how it was relatively unimportant in the decision of the mine workers at Luanshya to replace the system of tribal elders with a labor union, for the workers believed that a union would better represent their interests than the elders, who in many cases were not fully independent of the European management. However, the selection of union leaders was a matter in which Europeans were not involved, and electioneering and voting tended to follow ethnic lines. He suggests the principle of "situational selection," or the varying salience of ethnicity as a basis for social action across situations. Epstein argues that in the towns situations are specific, rather than diffuse, and individuals pattern their behavior across them. The key question is in which situations is ethnicity most important. Epstein proposes the hypothesis that in situations involving non-Africans, ethnicity is less important than in those cases where only Africans are involved.[28]

Assimilation versus Pluralism in Nairobi

Ethnicity is one of the most sensitive areas in most large African cities today, and therefore attitudes in this area are sometimes difficult to tap through survey research. At times subjects become suspicious, and at others they present what they believe to be the desired, rather than real, answers. For this reason, "unobtrusive" or indirect measures of ethnic identification or behaviors are especially useful.[29] In this study two types of indirect measures were developed. The first is designed to measure ethnic political identification, while the second was designed to tap the ethnic content of informal social networks.

Each respondent was asked how many ministers in the cabinet he could name, and then the first eight named were written down in the order named. The answer was then coded in terms of whether or not the first minister named was from the same tribe as the respondent. Table 4.1 shows that all ethnic groups in Nairobi named a minister from their own tribe more frequently than we would expect on a chance basis, although with the Abaluhya, a group long lacking a prominent leader, the percentage was not significantly higher. The figures in Table 4.2 are even more striking. This shows that the

Table 4.1. Percentage of Each Tribe Naming a Member of His Own Tribe First When Asked to Name Members of the Cabinet

	Tribe of Respondent				
	Kikuyu	Luo	Kamba	Baluhya	Other
Named Tribesman First	49%	54%	32%	14%	19%
Did Not Name Tribesman	51	46	68	86	81
	100%	100%	100%	100%	100%
Sample Size	(170)	(106)	(44)	(114)	(32)
Percentage of Cabinet	36%	18%	9%	9%	28%
Number in Cabinet	8	4	2	2	6

Table 4.2. Percent Naming Minister from Each Tribe by Tribe of Respondent

	Tribe of Ministers Named				
	Kikuyu	Luo	Kamba	Baluhya	Other
Respondent of Same Tribe	50%	33%	78%	76%	14%
Respondent of Different Tribe	50	67	22	24	86
	100%	100%	100%	100%	100%
Sample Size	(187)	(175)	(18)	(21)	(65)

Table 4.3. Percentage of Each Tribe Naming a Member of His Own Tribe First When Asked to Name His First Choice for the Next President by Tribe

	Tribe of Respondent				
	Kikuyu	Luo	Kamba	Baluhya	Tribe of Person Chosen
Named Tribesman	27%	65%	10%	8%	40%
Did Not Name Tribesman	73	35	90	92	60
	100%	100%	100%	100%	100%
Sample Size	(100)	(68)	(29)	(63)	(20)

Table 4.4. Percent Naming Presidential Choice from Each Tribe by Tribe of Respondent

	Kikuyu	Luo	Kamba	Baluhya	Other
Respondent of Same Tribe	63%	48%	100%	83%	6%
Respondent of Different Tribe	37	52	0	17	94
	100%	100%	100%	100%	100%
Sample Size	(43)	(92)	(3)	(6)	(136)

majority of times a minister was named he was named by a respondent of his own tribe. The one exception here was the Luo ministers, who were named by all tribes more frequently than by Luos alone. This is mainly because Tom Mboya was the person named most frequently among all the ministers, and the person most likely to be named if a respondent failed to name someone from his own tribe.

Second, each respondent was asked to name the person he would most like to see as the president of Kenya after Kenyatta. Table 4.3 shows that only among the Luo did a majority of the members of any tribe name another member of their tribe as their first choice. The following table (Table 4.4) shows, however, that among all the major tribal groups there was a strong tendency for individuals to name a member of their own tribe. The difference between the two tables is that two men, Vice-President Daniel arap Moi and Ronald Ngala, both of whom do not come from one of the major tribes, were named most frequently. However, when a person did mention a person from one of the major tribes, he tended to be a member of that tribal group.

The salience of ethnicity in social networks was measured by asking each respondent to think of his three best friends in the city and then to say from what district in Kenya they came. Since the home districts of the major tribes are ethnically homogeneous, an inference was made to the friend's tribe. Table 4.5 shows that the members of all major ethnic groups reported having a greater percentage of their closest friends from their own group than would be expected on a chance basis. The percentage having their closest friend from their birthplace is slightly lower for the Kikuyu and Luo and roughly the same for the other groups.

In accord with the detribalization hypothesis it is suggested that as African nations grow more industrial and urban, and as the population becomes more educated, that class divisions will become more salient than ethnic ones.[30] Underlying this notion is the assumption that stratification is based on either ethnicity or class. An alternative hypothesis is that both can serve as a basis of stratification, and that even the increasing class differences that are developing in the larger urban areas may occur along with ethnic stratification. In asserting that in America both stratification systems operate at the same time,

Table 4.5. Percentage of Each Tribe Reporting the Tribe of Their Closest Friend in the City

	Tribe of Respondent				
	Kikuyu	Luo	Kamba	Baluhya	Other
Closest Friend from Same Tribe	89%	86%	86%	80%	54%
Closest Friend from Different Tribe	11	14	14	20	46
	100%	100%	100%	100%	100%
Sample Size	(157)	(109)	(43)	(114)	(28)
Percent of City's Population	47%	15%	15%	16%	7%

Gordon has developed the term "ethclass."[31] Other American studies have shown the decreasing correlation between ethnic and class dimensions over time.[32]

Taking the above measures of ethnicity, we can now ask how they are related to several measures of detribalization: income, education, and length of residence in the city. A western education and a cash income expose the individual to new experiences—in Lerner's terms empathy is increased. In addition, attendance at school and the requirements of a job force individuals to adopt a series of behaviors different from their ancestors or relatives in the rural areas. Length of residence in the city should be important because it is a measure of how long an individual has been away from the tribal authority system and a part of the more general social subsystem of the tribe in the town.

Table 4.6 shows that having their closest friend from their own tribe or an ethnic political identification is unrelated to education, income, or any of the measures of length of residence in the city. This suggests that ethnic identification in politics and ethnicity as a basis for informal social organization are independent of social status as

Table 4.6. First Friend from Same Birthplace, Percentage of Friends from Same Birthplace, First Friend from Same Tribe, Percentage of Friends from Same Tribe, First Minister Named from Same Tribe, and First Choice for President from Same Tribe by Education, Income, Length of Residence, Percent of Life in City, and Percent of Life in City since Age 15

	(1)	(2)	(3)	(4)	(5)	(6)
Education	−.17* (464)	−.22* (467)	−.06 (446)	−.12* (457)	−.05 (461)	−.04 (278)
Income	−.16* (456)	−.21* (458)	−.08 (438)	−.16* (448)	−.02 (454)	−.04 (275)
Length of Residence	−.06 (458)	−.06 (471)	−.07 (450)	−.03 (461)	−.02 (465)	.01 (279)
Percent Life	−.13* (468)	−.13* (471)	−.07 (450)	−.04 (461)	−.02 (465)	.02 (279)
Percent Life +15	−.18* (468)	−.18* (471)	−.06 (450)	−.07 (461)	−.02 (465)	−.02 (279)

* Significant at the .01 level.
Same sizes in parentheses.
(1) Is first friend from same birthplace?
(2) Percentage of three friends from same birthplace.
(3) Is first friend same tribe as respondent?
(4) Percentage of three friends from same tribe.
(5) Is first minister named from same tribe as respondent?
(6) Is first choice for next president of Kenya from same tribe as respondent?

defined by education level and income. This is despite the fact that one reason often cited for the lack of mixing of ethnic groups at the lower income levels is the inability of individuals to communicate in any language except their vernacular or poor Swahili. Possessing this skill, however, does not seem to make any difference. Similarly length of residence or the proportion of one's life spent in the city is un-correlated with ethnicity, suggesting that while residence in the towns provides individuals with new skills and exposes them to a wider range of experiences, in areas where individuals exercise free choice, those with more urban experience are just as prone to choose friends from their own ethnic group or to have a high ethnic political identi-fication as the newly arrived migrant.

The data do show, however, a tendency for individuals with a higher education, income, and percent of their life spent in the city to have a lesser tendency to select their closest friends from their own birth-place, and for individuals with a higher education and income to have a higher percentage of their three friends from a tribe other than their own, although there is no correlation with their closest friend. Appar-ently, individuals with higher education and income do operate in a larger sphere of social interaction in selecting their secondary friends, but there is no difference insofar as their closest friend is concerned. There is also a negative relationship between education, income, and the percent of life spent in the city and the percentage of close friends from the respondent's birthplace. What seems to occur is that indi-viduals with higher social status and greater urban experience choose their friends from a wider group *within* their own ethnic community. There is a greater probability that an individual's closest friends were born in a different district, the higher his education, income, and the greater the percent of his life spent in the city. This suggests support for our contention that the perception of ethnicity is defined situation-ally, and that this definition takes new behavioral forms in different contexts. Thus, the greater the exposure to outside influences, the more likely an individual is to choose his closest friends from a broader base within his own ethnic community.

Political identifications are apparently unaffected by increasing exposure to either the city or new influences through either increased education or wealth. An individual's likelihood of naming a member of his own ethnic group as the first minister named or as his next choice for president is unaffected by his level of education, income, or urban experience. Certainly this suggests important limitations to the assimilationist position. Thus, greater exposure to new influences itself does not diminish ethnic political identification.

In interpreting these results it is important to keep in mind the distinction between acculturation and assimilation. In the former, the members of an ethnic group may lose distinctive social characteristics such as language, religion, food, or clothing which first mark a group when they come to the city. In the case of assimilation, in addition to developing new values the members of a group become fully integrated in the institutions of the wider society, as group and individual identification also diminish in importance. This is much less common, and all too often signs of acculturation are taken as indicators of assimilation. Our data here show clearly how increased acculturation does not automatically lead either to assimilation or to diminished ethnic identification. The consequences of this are that new markers of ethnicity may develop in urban situations which allow it to retain a vitality and importance in political and social life.[33]

It is not just the newly arrived migrant in the city who behaves as a "tribalist." Among the elite, friendship networks are often tribally homogeneous. In Nairobi there does not seem to be more entertaining of Luos by Kikuyus (and vice versa) at the university level than there is in some of the low-income housing estates. Social networks within the city are based to a great extent on kinship and ethnicity at all socioeconomic levels.

Political Implications
The first section of this chapter described several alternative approaches to the relationship between cultural assimilation and ethnic identification. Migrants to large cities tend to develop new cultural patterns as they leave their areas of origin and withdraw from the traditional authority system. The term detribalization has been applied to this phenomenon in Africa and assimilation in the United States. It has often been assumed, but rarely tested, that this phenomenon is associated with a decrease in ethnicity as a basis for social and political organization.

Data presented here, and elsewhere, suggest that exactly the opposite is the case. Even with cultural assimilation—increased education, income, and urban experience—individuals in Nairobi tend to have friendship networks and ethnic political identifications that are just as strong as those persons who have not experienced these cultural changes, although the base from which they select their friends grows larger. Ethnicity, as a basis for social and political organization, should continue to be important in urban politics. Even with increased education and further cultural change, its importance will not diminish. At times it may provide the basis for violence. In other cases it may pose difficulties for getting individuals to consider themselves part of a nation whose membership is compatible with their tribal loyalty.

Ethnicity, however, does not just provide a basis for division within a society. It also serves as an integrating factor.[34] Migrants first arriving in Nairobi enter immediately into an ethnically based friendship network, rather than having to develop entirely new ties upon arrival in town. In the sample cited earlier, 85 percent of the individuals interviewed said that they stayed with either a relative or fellow tribesman when they first came to Nairobi. The remainder either lived in employer housing, stayed with a friend they made in the city, or had a place of their own. The literature on West African cities places great stress upon the role of the voluntary organizations in assimilating newer immigrants into town life. What is missing, however, is a comparison of voluntary organizations with other agencies of socialization. In Nairobi, the formal organizations are far less important than the friends and relatives a person knows. If a man is well educated, he can often find a job on his own; otherwise he tries to have relatives or friends with employment find out if there is a job available where they are working.

Strong ethnic ties provide the basis for the only social security system that most African countries can afford at the present time. When individuals experience financial difficulties, it is their relatives and their tribesmen who help them out. Since independence many individuals in Nairobi have started small welfare or cooperative societies. As a number of these groups are not formally chartered by the government and regulated by the Ministry of Cooperatives, government figures greatly underestimate the number of these organizations in

Nairobi. A man who loses his job can always eat his meals with relatives or tribesmen whom he knows. If this were not the case, the government would have a serious problem on its hands as there are many unemployed people in the city.

The maintenance of strong ethnic ties should also ease the transition from tribal to urban society. Individuals associating with people from the same place at home feel greater social trust than they would with strangers from the town. They can relax by speaking their own language or eating special foods. While their children, born in town, may behave differently in this regard, they still will maintain strong ethnic identification, even though they never lived in their father's home area.[35]

An important change taking place in African social systems is the increased role differentiation, or independence of social roles, found in the urban areas. One result is that individuals may maintain a high ethnic identification in one sphere of activity, while ethnicity has a very low salience in others. Role differentiation, or compartmentalization of life's activities, and the growing specificity of activities in the urban areas mean that neither ethnicity nor any other single factor is likely to be the sole basis for social stratification.

Class and Ethnicity in Nairobi
Ethnicity is a powerful predictor of friendship choices and political identification in Nairobi but not the only basis on which an urban social and political system can be stratified. As long as ethnic identification and ties are only moderately strong, other factors such as occupation, education level, or religion also operate. Often several principles may operate together and are not necessarily in conflict with one another. At the same time it is possible to assess the relative importance of different principles, such as class and ethnicity.[36]

To evaluate the relative importance of class and ethnicity, we return briefly to our data on friendship choices in the city. Each respondent was asked where in the city his closest friend lived. Since the neighborhoods in the city are generally homogeneous by rent and associated with particular income and education levels of residents, each neighborhood was scored in terms of being a lower-, middle-, or upper-class community, and then each friendship choice was scored in terms of whether or not the respondent's friend had the same class background as he did. The data (Table 4.7) show that while both class and ethnicity are important in the selection of close friends, their contribution is not equal. The number of friends selected outside a person's ethnic group is about four times smaller than the number from outside his social class.[37]

This relative ranking of ethnicity and class certainly can change over time, and we need to understand better the forces that might operate to increase the importance of either or both factors. In addition, it should be pointed out that the relative importance of ethnicity and class in the selection of friends may not hold across other spheres of activity. In particular, in the following chapters our data show that status considerations are of far greater importance, for example, in predicting levels of political involvement and interest, while ethnic membership is a better predictor of political orientations toward the government.

Table 4.7. Ethnicity and Class in the Selection of Closest Friend in Nairobi

| | Ethnicity of Closest Friend | |
	Same as Respondent	Different from Respondent
Class of Closest Friend Same as Respondent	43% (190)	11% (47)
Different from Respondent	40% (176)	6% (26)

Sample sizes in parentheses.

Part **II** Political Life in Nairobi

Chapter 5   Attitudes about Politics and Politicians after Independence

Introduction

Kenya attained political independence in 1963, less than a decade after the colonial government permitted widespread African political participation. The Kenya African Naional Union (KANU), which led the country to independence, was formed in 1960 at the end of the state of emergency, originally declared in 1952. With Jomo Kenyatta at its head, and with strong support from the Kikuyu and the Luo, the two largest tribes in Kenya, KANU had little trouble winning control of the government.[1]

The excitement generated among African during the independence struggle is hard to imagine a decade later. The issue of independence was simple, straightforward, and highly charged emotionally. It pitted the nationalist leaders against the colonial power. A leader could easily catalogue the injustices and abuses of the colonial government and promise that an African government would end them. In Kenya, as in most other African countries, the independence leaders, Kenyatta, Tom Mboya, Oginga Odinga, James Gichuru, and others effectively manipulated a small number of highly emotive symbols to mobilize support from the population.

Politics quickly changed as Kenya entered the postindependence period. The opposition party at the time of independence, the Kenya African Democratic Union (KADU) dissolved itself and joined KANU in 1964. Soon after, however, new political divisions erupted within KANU, and in 1966 Odinga led 29 members of parliament (MPs) out of the party and formed the Kenya People's Union (KPU). Odinga is an important Luo leader, and KPU received its greatest support from among the Luo in western Kenya, thus shattering the uneasy coalition of Kenya's two largest ethnic groups in the ruling party. By 1969 KPU was declared illegal, and most of its important leaders were placed in detention.

If the independence era can be characterized in terms of the politics of participation, the postindependence period is typified by the politics of administration. Today's issues are more complex and less emotional. The goals of African governments are broader and at the same time less realizable. The abstract idea of economic development cannot arouse a population to the same fervor as the idea of independence, when economic changes are so slow and the path to them so unsure. People were frequently reinforced during the independence era as they saw their actions achieve the desired changes: Africans gained an increasing amount of political power in a relatively short period of time. Today's successes, such as the opening of a new hospital or school, are far less dramatic and not frequent enough to sustain a large number of people whose aspirations have grown many times faster than the resources of their governments.

Increasingly people are more uncertain of the leaders they once supported so unhesitatingly. The gap between leaders and followers widens as political officials are charged with having "forgotten about the people who first elected them." Few elected leaders are easily available to their constituents. In Nairobi, for example, three of the eight MPs are now serving as cabinet members. Others are busy with their jobs. "As soon as they had their first glass of wine and good meal, they forgot about the people," said one informant. "They never visit here any more." At the same time the gap in the standard of living between the politicians and the mass of the people has become more obvious. The politicians have become *Wabenzi* (men who drive Mercedes-Benz and other large cars). President Kenyatta's behavior symbolizes much of the change. Whenever the president travels in the country, a large number of police and other security men accompany him, clearing the roads well before the presidential motorcade, and surrounding him to prevent crowds from getting close. To a westerner, particularly an American, this sort of precaution on the part of a head of state, particularly a man over 75 years of age, seems quite reasonable; but to a number of Kenyans it symbolizes an increasing social distance between themselves and their government. Before the annual TANU Party Conference several years ago, Tanzania's President Nyerere marched over 125 miles from his home to Mwanza to stress the necessity for Tanzanians to be "self-reliant." This had a great impact in Nairobi, where a number of people said to the author, "Why can't Kenyatta do that?" At first we responded, "Probably because he is over 75 years old." To which the reply always was, "We don't want him to walk that far, we just want him to walk *with* us, *like* us."

While the politicians continue to tell Kenyans that they must work hard and sacrifice in order to achieve development, few are convinced that the politicians are sacrificing very much themselves. On the contrary, there is the widespread belief that they are using their positions to acquire greater property and material possessions. Talk of corruption is increasing, and the government seems to have made only half-hearted efforts to root it out. On one day the vice-president told parliament that corruption was increasing and the government was determined to end it; the next day he spoke at a political rally where he charged that certain people were spreading rumors about corruption in Kenya and that if they did not stop they would be detained. But even if one ignores corruption in Kenya, the salaries the politicians receive are large and the business connections most have developed since attaining public office are impressive indeed.

Two general and important political questions in Kenya in the postindependence period concern political succession after President Kenyatta dies or retires and the politicization of ethnicity. With no clear successor to Kenyatta, there has been a great deal of factional jockeying within KANU. Until his assassination in 1969, Tom Mboya, a Luo, was the most dominant political figure after the president, and any discussion of succession always considered his position. His death intensified speculation about other political figures, and at the same time sharpened already strong tribal differences, most clearly dividing the Kikuyu, who dominate the government, from the Luo, who are most clearly associated with the opposition. Increasingly, jobs, housing, and other valuables are distributed to individuals according to criteria other than ability or need. There is usually a strong relationship between the tribe of the head of a government department and the tribe of the majority of the employees in that department. Much of the blame is placed on the Kikuyus, clearly the dominant tribe in both the city and central governments, but it is evident that this practice is engaged in by members of other tribes and not just as a defense against the Kikuyu. Clearly, the problem is deeper in that it pits one set of values, allegiance to family and clan, against the values of impersonality and achievement, which are important in the modern economic system.

The data presented in this chapter outline the distribution of political attitudes in Nairobi in the postindependence period, showing

differences between the major ethnic groups on such specific questions
as the perception of improvement in living conditions since independence and the problems of tribalism and corruption, as well as on
general orientations of estrangement and powerlessness. The Kikuyu
have a more positive orientation toward the present regime than do the
Luo, but while the documentation of this fact is interesting, it is not
particularly startling. At the same time, there is variation *within* each
group, and when we consider how the life-style and social status of
individuals are related to their political attitudes, the data show that
their effects are not the same for individuals within each ethnic group.
Ethnicity, in other words, intervenes in the relationship between life-
style or social status and political attitudes, as the Kikuyu and Luo
provide different participation opportunities and social support for
the formation and expression of political beliefs by group members.

Political Attitudes after Independence
There is disillusionment and disappointment with politicians and
government in many sectors since independence, but few Africans
would go so far as to say that things were better under the colonial
government. Rather, they say that things did not turn out as well as
they had hoped they would. There is also a widespread belief that
politics is a dirty game in which people play for high stakes—often for
the lives of the participants. In the same way that the idea of independence rapidly spread across the continent during the previous decade,
today the specter of military coups and political assassinations has
taken its place. Leaders know that their positions are tenuous but
are too comfortable to leave them. Nonpoliticians, on the other hand,
are often afraid of becoming involved because of the personal risk
they perceive.

Disillusionment with politics and condemnation of the behavior of
politicians are not universal characteristics of Nairobi politics today.
Some people, in fact, are quite satisfied with the government. They
realize that there has been a vast increase of expenditure in the public
sector for such services as health and education. Outpatient care at
Kenyan hospitals and clinics, for example, is now free, and primary
school, while not free, is available to many more children than at any
time during the colonial period. In addition, there is more economic

opportunity for Africans entering the business sector or for those planting cash crops.

Each respondent was asked to evaluate the extent to which his own personal living conditions and living conditions in the city had improved since independence.[2] Table 5.1 shows that the overwhelming majority thought that both the conditions in the city and their own conditions had either improved or remained the same since independence. Only about 10 percent felt that conditions had grown worse since *uhuru*.[3]

Given the importance of tribal identification and antagonism in Kenyan politics, it is expected that there will be significant differences between the major tribes in their perception of the degree to which living conditions have changed since independence. Table 5.2 gives the mean scores of each group, and it shows that the Kikuyu perceive the

Table 5.1. Perception of Degree of Improvement in Living Conditions in the City and Personal Living Conditions since Independence

	Living Conditions in the City	Personal Living Conditions
Improved	68%	52%
Remained the Same or Don't Know	24	36
Grown Worse	8	12
	100%	100%
Sample Size	498	498

Table 5.2. Mean Scores on Questions concerning Improvement of Living Conditions in the City, Personal Living Conditions, and Degree to Which Government Has Lived up to Expectations by Tribe

	Living Conditions in City* (1)	Living Conditions Personal* (2)	More or Less Done than Expected* (3)
Kikuyu	2.79 (179)	2.62 (179)	2.22 (179)
Luo	2.42 (114)	2.29 (114)	1.88 (113)
Luhya	2.50 (126)	2.33 (126)	2.00 (124)
Kamba	2.45 (46)	2.15 (46)	2.03 (46)
Other Groups	2.58 (33)	2.48 (33)	2.06 (33)
TOTAL	2.59 (498)	2.42 (498)	2.06 (495)

* Group differences are significant at the .01 level. The higher the score, the higher the level of satisfaction.

greatest improvement in living conditions in the city since independence, while the Luo see the least improvement. Likewise the Kikuyu
also believe that there has been the greatest improvement in living
conditions on the personal level, while the Kamba, Luo, and Luhya
perceive the least improvement. The Kikuyu are more satisfied that
the government has done at least as much as they expected it would
do when it took office, while the Luos are relatively less satisfied.[4] The
scores of the other groups are between those of these two tribes.

The perception of the degree of improvement in living conditions
since independence both in the city and on a personal level should be
related to an individual's position in the social structure of Nairobi.
Specifically we expect to find the following relationships:

(1) those individuals with the most favorable positions in the social
    structure, that is, those people with the highest level of education
    and with the highest income should perceive their situations
    most favorably and should perceive the greatest degree of improve-
    ment in living conditions; and

(2) those individuals with the most pressure from their families in the
    rural areas, specifically those people who send money home most
    frequently, and those with the greatest number of rural relatives
    visiting them in the city should perceive the least improvement in
    their own living conditions and in the living conditions in the
    city in general.

Individuals with high levels of education and a high income are in
the best position to move into good jobs and find business opportunities in the city since independence. They are most likely to have
replaced the members of the European and Asian communities in
government jobs, and most likely to have used their incomes either to
begin businesses or to purchase large farms. On the other hand, people
without these advantages are the least likely to have benefited from
the changes that have taken place since *uhuru*.

Relatives in the rural areas often make a wide variety of demands
upon the urban dweller. Many of the demands center around the
payment of school fees to take advantage of the widespread expansion
of primary education in recent years. Rural relatives also burden the
Nairobian by coming to the city and living in his usually already over-
crowded accommodations untl they can find a job and a place of their

own. Therefore, it is expected that persons with the highest level of contact with the rural areas will perceive the smallest improvement in living conditions since independence.

The data in Table 5.3 show that the first hypothesis is confirmed, while the second is rejected because the relationship is exactly the opposite of the one hypothesized. The perception of the degree of improvement in living conditions since independence in both the city and on the personal level is positively related to education and income. The higher the level of education and income, the greater improvement in living conditions perceived. The relationship is significant for both the Kikuyu and Luo subsamples, and among the Kikuyu landownership is also related to the degree of improvement in living conditions. Those Kikuyu with no land and those with the smallest holdings perceive the least degree of improvement in living conditions since independence, while among the Luo there are no differences by landownership or the size of landholdings.

Contrary to our second hypothesis, the higher the level of contact with the rural areas (and looking at the specific individual measures of contact, the more money sent home), the greater the perception of improved living conditions. Apparently, the individuals with the highest contact perceive the highest degree of improvement, despite

Table 5.3. Degree of Improvement in Living Conditions in the City and on the Personal Level since Independence by Education, Income, Landownership, Size of Farm, and Contact with the Rural Areas Index by Tribe

	Kikuyu		Luo		Total Sample	
	Condi-tions in City	Personal Condi-tions	Condi-tions in City	Personal Condi-tions	Condi-tions in City	Personal Condi-tions
Education	.21* (179)	.12† (179)	.23† (114)	.31* (114)	.21* (492)	.17* (492)
Income	.20* (175)	.19* (175)	.23† (111)	.33* (111)	.19* (484)	.24* (484)
Landowner	.18† (179)	.17† (179)	.05 (113)	.04 (113)	.01 (497)	.04 (497)
Size of Land-holding	.18† (178)	.17† (178)	.00 (113)	.12 (113)	.03 (497)	.08 (498)
Contact with Rural Areas Index	.28* (179)	.25* (179)	.05 (114)	.12 (114)	.13* (498)	.14* (498)

* Significant at the .01 level.
† Significant at the .05 level.
Sample sizes in parentheses.

the fact that their high contact is associated with a higher level of
demands for assistance from rural relatives (manifest through behaviors
such as sending money home more frequently). Contact with the rural
areas, however, is affected by social status. That is, individuals with
the highest incomes and highest levels of education are those with the
highest levels of contact.[5] Partialing for the effects of income lowers the
relationship between contact with the rural areas and the perception
of improvement in living conditions in both the city and on a personal
level to the point where they are no longer significant for the entire
sample, although they do remain significant for the Kikuyu subgroup.

Thus, the perception of the degree of improvement in living conditions is affected by ethnicity. Generally, the Kikuyu perceive a greater
degree of improvement in living conditions since independence than
the Luo. Among both groups, social status factors, education, and
income explain differences in the perception of improvements. In
addition, among the Kikuyu landownership in the rural areas and
contact with the rural areas were positively related to the degree of
improvement perceived.

Since independence, probably the most potentially explosive attitudes are those surrounding the question of "tribalism." Although they
are used in a variety of contexts, tribalism and brotherization refer
essentially to the mobilization of ethnic sentiments (or even more
localized bases such as clan or subclan) for advancement in politics or
business. It refers to the practice of filling a government vacancy with
a member of a particular tribe when there are clearly better-qualified
candidates from other groups, or to the practice of awarding loans on
the basis of family connections and ethnic loyalty rather than merit.
It generally means the division of the political spoils on the basis of
tribal membership.

At one time, transethnic appeals were strong in Nairobi politics. In
the early 1960s Tom Mboya, for example, campaigned as a candidate
who could represent the interests of his constituents regardless of their
tribe. In 1961, running against a blatantly pro-Kikuyu candidate who
campaigned on tribal lines, Mboya won an overwhelming victory in
Nairobi. It is very doubtful whether any candidate today, including
President Kenyatta, could be similarly successful.

Feelings have hardened a good deal in those few years. Kikuyus, whose movements in and out of Nairobi were curbed during the Emergency, have poured into the city since independence, giving members of other groups the impression that Nairobi is a Kikuyu city and that other tribes are only temporary visitors. Similarly, Kikuyu have moved quickly to seize the power positions in both the national and city governments, and they are far and away the most numerous among African businessmen throughout Kenya, as they move into positions vacated by Asians leaving the country. Finally, there is a feeling of frustration on the part of other groups as government funds are poured into Kikuyu-dominated Central Province to maintain government hospitals, schools, and other services that are far skimpier in other areas of Kenya.[6]

Until now the reaction of the Kikuyu has been to solidify their positions further, apparently oblivious to the great level of hatred and anxiety directed at them. Their reaction is that they have a right to the fruits of independence more than other groups because they did more to fight for independence than anyone else. They assert that they are ready to fight again for the defense of their gains. The reaction of other groups, with the exception of KPU, has been, for the most part, unorganized. At the same time resentment against the Kikuyu is building up. Large numbers of Luo, Luhya, and Kamba are despondent because they see jobs, promotions, trading licenses, and loans awarded on the basis of tribal membership rather than ability, and they see no immediate prospect for changing the situation.

In order to examine the extent to which different ethnic groups evaluate the problem of tribalism differently, each respondent was asked the following three questions:[7]

1. In your opinion how serious is the problem of government officials and politicians doing special favors for their relatives and close friends? Very serious . . . 1 Serious . . . 2 Not important . . . 3

2. Some people think that politicians are helping to eliminate the problem of tribalism in Kenya; others suggest that they are stirring up tribal differences. Which do you think is most true? Trying to eliminate tribalism . . . 1 They are doing both . . . 2 Stirring up differences . . . 3

3. How serious a problem do you think tribalism is in Nairobi today? Very serious. . . 1 Serious . . . 2 Not important . . . 3

The three items are highly interrelated and were combined to make up an index that measured the respondent's evaluation of how important a problem tribalism in politics is today in Nairobi. Three-quarters of the population considers tribalism to be a very serious or a serious problem in postindependence Kenya and sees the politicians as making it more serious. As Table 5.4 shows, however, the tribal groups in Nairobi differ significantly in their evaluations of the problem of tribalism. As is expected, the Kikuyu consider it to be less serious, and the Luo see it as more serious than the average. The same pattern holds for each of the individual questions, as well as for the combined index.

Our argument to this point has stressed that ethnicity is a good predictor of attitudes toward the government, but it should be realized that it is not the only one, and other variables are likely to be associated with variation in attitudes within each group as well. Ethnic groups may achieve relative unity on certain questions, but at the same time there are often important factional differences within a group, and total attitudinal consensus is rarely found.

To illustrate this point, data are presented in Table 5.5 to show the effect of ethnicity and class on individual perceptions of personal improvement in living conditions since independence. While the

Table 5.4. Mean Scores for Perceptions of the Seriousness of Tribalism as a Problem by Tribe*

	Problem of Special Favors†	Problem of Tribalism†	Politicians Stirring up Differences†	Total Index†
Kikuyu	2.01 (179)	1.89 (179)	1.76 (179)	5.66 (179)
Kamba	2.24 (46)	2.02 (46)	1.99 (45)	6.25 (46)
Baluhya	2.23 (126)	2.18 (125)	1.82 (126)	6.23 (126)
Luo	2.20 (114)	2.21 (114)	2.25 (114)	6.66 (114)
Other	2.18 (33)	1.94 (33)	2.03 (33)	6.15 (33)
Total	2.14 (498)	2.05 (497)	2.02 (498)	6.21 (498)

Sample sizes in parentheses.
* A high score on each of the first two items and on the total index means that tribalism and doing special favors are regarded as very serious problems; a high score on the third item indicates support for the view that politicians are stirring up tribal differences.
† Group differences significant at the .01 level.

Table 5.5. Mean Scores on Perception of Individual Improvement in Living Conditions since Independence

Tribe of Respondent	Social Class of Respondent			Total
	Lower	Middle	Upper	
Kikuyu	2.5 (71)	2.7 (57)	2.7 (51)	2.6 (179)
Kamba	2.1 (24)	2.2 (19)	2.3 (3)	2.2 (46)
Baluhya	2.0 (45)	2.6 (47)	2.4 (34)	2.3 (126)
Luo	2.0 (44)	2.4 (45)	2.6 (25)	2.3 (114)
Total	2.2 (198)*	2.5 (178)*	2.6 (122)*	2.4 (498)*

Sample sizes in parentheses.
* The column totals also include 33 respondents from other ethnic groups.
The higher the score, the more favorable the view of changes since independence.

Kikuyu are more likely to have a favorable attitude than the Luo, at the same time, upper-class Luo see changes as more favorable than do lower-class Kikuyu. The attitudes of working-class Kikuyu on this question are closer to those of upper-class Luhya and Luo than to those of upper-class Kikuyu. Similarly, upper-class Kamba, Luhya, and Luo are closer to lower-class Kikuyu than to the lower classes in their own ethnic groups. In short, responses to government within ethnic groups in Nairobi are not homogeneous, although ethnicity acts as a crucial intervening variable. In the following section we will turn to some of the mechanisms underlying this relationship.

Estrangement from Politics

As expected, attitudes about changes in living conditions since independence and the problem of corruption and tribalism are related to ethnicity in postindependence Nairobi. We expect to find similar results in considering political estrangement, an individual's feeling that the government and authorities are unable or unwilling to serve the interests of people like himself.

Estrangement is more than simply a dislike of particular politicians or disapproval of government policy. It is a more general orientation that views the government and the authorities as either serving their own narrow interests or acting under the control of a small clique that neglects the general welfare. Estrangement is particularly prominent among ethnic, religious, and regional groups, especially in developing countries, although it may also be associated with low social status positions as well.

In Nairobi, the effects of ethnicity on estrangement are strong, as is shown in Table 5.6.[8] The data show that the Kikuyu are significantly less estranged than the Luo, as expected, and that virtually no social status or life-style variables are related to political estrangement until tribal differences are taken into account (Table 5.7).

Controlling for the effects of tribe and looking at the correlations between social structure and estrangement *within* the Kikuyu and Luo groups reveal some interesting differences between them. To show these, we begin with three hypotheses suggesting how position in the social structure should be related to estrangement and then examine

Table 5.6. Political Estrangement by Tribe

	Mean Scores on Estrangement Index
Kikuyu	9.3 (179)
Kamba	10.2 (46)
Baluhya	10.3 (126)
Luo	10.7 (114)
Other	10.3 (33)
Total	10.0 (498)

Sample sizes in parentheses.
F-ratio is significant at the .001 level.

Table 5.7. Political Estrangement by Education, Income, Landownership, Cinema Attendance, Contact with the Rural Areas, Amount of Time Spent Home, Frequency of Visits Home, and Formal Group Membership by Tribe

	Kikuyu	Luo	Total Sample
Education	.25* (179)	.06 (114)	.10† (492)
Income	.18† (175)	.09 (111)	.07 (484)
Landowner	−.20* (179)	.06 (113)	−.05 (497)
Attended Cinema	.14† (176)	.18† (114)	.06 (494)
Contact with the Rural Areas	−.11 (179)	.21† (114)	−.03 (498)
Time Spent Home in Past Year	−.23* (177)	.09 (111)	−.02 (493)
How Often Home in Past Year	−.19* (177)	.28* (111)	−.02 (492)
Formal Group Membership	−.03 (179)	.18† (114)	.06 (498)

* Significant at the .01 level.
† Significant at the .05 level.
Sample sizes in parentheses.

the data which show that each variable has a different effect for the two groups:

(1) those individuals with the most favorable positions in the social structure, that is, those with the highest levels of education and income, and the largest landholdings, should be least estranged from the government;

(2) the higher the level of contact maintained with the rural areas, the greater the pressure for support an individual is likely to perceive and the more estranged he will become from the government because of his situation; and

(3) the greater the number of voluntary associations of which an individual is a member, the more likely he will be to develop a set of social contacts that can assist him with his difficulties and the less likely he is to feel estranged.

Individuals in the most disadvantaged positions in society, that is, those people with lower education and income or without land, should be more disillusioned with the government than others as they stand to benefit the most by increases in governmental social services. Individuals with higher education or landholdings, on the other hand, shoud be in a better position to take care of themselves. People with the highest level of contact with the rural areas should receive directly or indirectly the greatest number of requests for assistance from their families in the rural areas. Therefore, they should be most disillusioned about the current political situation and most likely to support a change in policies, such as the implementation of a program of free primary education, because requests for assistance from the rural areas often revolve around the payment of children's school fees. The third hypothesis relates estrangement to membership in formal groups. Individuals who are members of voluntary associations in the city are able to turn to these groups for assistance and companionship and should be less estranged than others who do not have this alternative.

Among the Kikuyu and Luo, none of these hypotheses is completely supported by the data present in Table 5.7. In addition, none of the relationships is in the same direction for the two, showing that different social conditions are related to the development of feelings of estrangement among each group.

The first hypothesis suggests that low income and lack of education

and land are related to feelings of high estrangement. Among the Luo
there is no relationship between any of these measures of social status
and estrangement, while among the Kikuyu all three are significant
but not in the same direction. Kikuyus who are highly educated and
have high incomes are *more* likely to be estranged than those with low
education and income, while at the same time those who do not own
any land in the rural areas are more estranged than those who do.
Thus, estrangement is positively related to education and income and
negatively to land ownership. Among both groups individuals who
have attended the cinema in downtown Nairobi in the past year are
more estranged than those who have not, suggesting that, contrary to
expectations, feelings of estrangement are positively related to access
to favorable positions in society.

The effect of contact with the rural areas is in the opposite direction
for the two groups. Among the Luo the relationship is as hypothesized.
Those with higher contact with the rural areas, especially those who
travel home most frequently, are most estranged, while among the
Kikuyu those who have spent the greatest amount of time home in the
past year and those who travel home most frequently are the *least*
estranged. This striking difference in the effect of the same variable
among the two groups suggests that a different mechanism may be
operating than the degree of pressure for assistance from the rural
family, which we first suggested. Instead, it appears that the greater
the contact with the rural areas, and particularly, the more frequently
an individual visits home, the more likely he is to hold the views
toward the government which are dominant in his home area. This
means that Kikuyus with a high level of contact with the rural
areas are less estranged from the government than those with low
contact, while among the Luos the relationship is the reverse, and high
contact is associated with high estrangement.

Formal group membership[9] is unrelated to feelings of political estrangement among the Kikuyu, while among the Luo the data show
that contrary to our prediction, formal group membership is positively
related to estrangement, especially among those who are members of
a welfare, district, or tribal association, such as the Luo Union. The
mechanism may be the same as for contact with the rural areas among
the Luo. Apparently those Luos who maintain the strongest ties with

their families in Nyanza and those who participate most in voluntary associations, especially welfare, district, or tribal associations, which tend to be ethnically homogeneous, hold the dominant norm of their tribal group, a rejection of the policies of the current government and disaffection from the current politicians. Contact with the rural areas and formal group membership bring them into contact with other members of the Luo community, especially those from western Kenya around Kisumu, where there is a great deal of support for both Odinga and KPU.

The same mechanism might be expected to work in the opposite direction for the Kikuyu, but we find no relationship between formal group membership and estrangement for them. One possible hypothesis is that associational life is less important for the Kikuyu than for the Luo. This is certainly consistent with the work of Parkin[10] as well as with the popular images that Luos have stronger associational ties in East African cities than Bantu groups, such as the Buganda or Kikuyu. Our data suggest that this is not fully accurate in Nairobi, where Kikuyus are not significantly less likely than Luos to be members of voluntary associations. At the same time, there are significant differences between the groups when not just the total number of memberships but also the *types* of organizations are considered. Luos are far more likely than Kikuyus to participate in clan, tribal, or welfare associations, while the reverse is the case for trade unions and political parties. Ethnic associations could well be expected to foster the transmission of a particular view of the government, as opposed to trade unions, which are multiethnic and have a carefully guarded relationship with the government or political party branches, which are virtually inactive in the city. Thus, this relationship seems to be more a function of the type of Luo associational ties than of their mere existence.

Feelings of estrangement are related to the perception of the importance of tribalism and corruption as political problems. Estrangement is part of a cluster of political attitudes that appear to reinforce each other both in the total sample and within each ethnic group. The higher the level of estrangement, the less likely individuals are to perceive improvement in living conditions or in their own lives since independence, the more likely they are to accuse politicians of abusing

Table 5.8. Estrangement by Perception of Improvement in Living Standard in the City and on a Personal Level since Independence, Tribalism Items, and Should Opposition Party Exist by Tribe

	Total Sample	Kikuyu	Luo
Living conditions in city improved?	−.35* (498)	−.20* (179)	−.31* (114)
Living conditions—personal—improved?	−.35* (498)	−.33* (179)	−.18† (114)
How serious the problem of government officials doing special favors for their close friends and relatives?	.33* (498)	.20* (179)	.43* (114)
Are politicians stirring up tribal differences or trying to eliminate tribalism?	.31* (498)	.22* (179)	.24* (114)
How serious a problem is tribalism in Nairobi today?	.25* (497)	.12 (178)	.25* (114)
Should Kenya have an opposition party these days?	.32* (496)	.30* (178)	.33* (114)

* Significant at the .01 level.
† Significant at the .05 level.
Sample sizes in parentheses.

their positions for personal gain, the more likely they are to consider tribalism a serious problem in Nairobi, and the more likely they are to feel that the politicians stir up tribal differences rather than work to eliminate them. Last, estrangement is positively associated with the belief that the country should have an opposition political party.

Although estrangement is related to different social variables within each tribal group, there are almost no differences between the Kikuyu and Luo in the correlations between the attitude questions and estrangement, as is seen in Table 5.8. Despite the differences in the level of estrangement between the Kikuyu and Luo, the relationship between this belief and other attitudes is the same within each group.

Political Powerlessness
Individuals differ widely in their perception of their own ability to be effective politically. Some take an essentially deterministic view of their social and political universe and believe that there is relatively little that the single individual can do to produce changes, while others see their environment as subject to manipulation and control

through individual action. We call such attitudes, respectively, feelings of political powerlessness and feelings of political efficacy.

Studies in a variety of settings indicate that feelings of powerlessness are most commonly found among individuals occupying positions of relative deprivation in the social structure. Thus, individuals with the smallest available resources for altering their social situation are those who most commonly believe that there is little that individuals can do to effect change. For example, individuals who are relatively uneducated are least prepared to understand the complex activities of modern bureaucracy and least able to deal successfully with bureaucracy when a problem comes up in their lives. Therefore, they are least likely to perceive it as subject to individual manipulation.

Traditional belief systems that consider the individual as living in an environment which he cannot manipulate or control also support feelings of individual powerlessness. The process of modernization or social change, according to writers such as Lerner,[11] is the acquisition by individuals of the skills that permit them to conceptualize their social environment in terms of alternative choices. Of particular importance is the spread of literacy and the mass media, both of which present the individual with detailed images of social life outside of his immediate experience. He begins to develop abstract modes of thought and to conceive of wider ranges of social choice. Lerner's work draws particular attention to the development of a sense of "empathy," the ability to put oneself in someone else's position, the ability to identify with people and situations beyond one's personal experience.

These two views about the origin of feelings of political powerlessness are not necessarily incompatible with each other, and in some ways are complementary. For example, education is a resource that provides skills to assist individuals in coping with many of the problems facing them in their daily lives in a city such as Nairobi. On the simplest level, it permits the intake of large amounts of information through printed matter, such as newspapers or magazines. At the same time it is seen as crucial in the modernization process because it helps to free individuals from traditional beliefs of personal powerlessness.

In order to test these views, we have correlated our index of political powerlessness with four variables that measure either relative deprivation in the social structure or exposure to new ideas: landownership in the rural areas, income, education level, and cinema attendance. Landownership is an important measure of a person's social position in the rural community, and since so few residents of Nairobi are totally willing to cut ties with the rural areas, landownership should be negatively related to feelings of powerlessness. Likewise, income as a measure of social position in the urban community should be negatively related to this attitude. Education is a measure both of social status and of exposure to new ideas, and the higher the level of education, the greater the expected sense of political efficacy. Cinema attendance is measured by asking people if they had attended a movie in downtown Nairobi in the past year. It indicates an exposure to outside ideas but also is an indirect measure of social status because movies shown in the center of the city are in English.

These hypotheses are unevenly supported by the data presented in Table 5.9, which show that the pattern is not parallel for the Kikuyu and Luo. For the whole sample, education and cinema attendance are significantly related to powerlessness in the predicted direction, while income and landownership are not.[12] All of the correlations are very low, however.

When tribe is controlled, the data show that lack of land is especially important in predicting feelings of political powerlessness among the Kikuyu. A great deal of attention has been placed upon the role of landownership among the Kikuyu since the beginning of the colonial period, and the finding here supports the view that a man's lack of land, even a small holding, symbolizes a great failure. His inability to acquire land is apparently related to beliefs stressing his inability to act efficaciously. This finding also underscores the importance of the

Table 5.9. Political Powerlessness by Landownership, Income, Education Level, and Cinema Attendance by Tribe

	Total Sample	Kikuyu	Luo
Landownership	−.05 (497)	−.17† (179)	.04 (113)
Income	−.04 (484)	.00 (175)	−.07 (111)
Education Level	−.09† (492)	−.01 (179)	−.17† (114)
Cinema Attendance	−.11* (494)	.00 (176)	−.26* (114)

* Significant at the .01 level.
† Significant at the .05 level.
Sample sizes in parentheses.

link between land and politics, particularly among the Kikuyu, where political leaders and movements have consistently built up support by promising to provide land for the landless and to restore alienated lands to their Kikuyu owners.

Cinema attendance and education are negatively related to feelings of powerlessness among the Luo. Exposure to new ideas through the mass media and formal education are important in developing feelings of political efficacy. At the same time, income and landownership, which are organized differently among the Luo than among the Kikuyu, are unrelated to feelings of political powerlessness.

Unlike estrangement, the other dimension of political alienation, powerlessness is not related to other political attitudes.[13] Interestingly, the largest correlation in Table 5.10 shows that while estrangement and powerlessness are unrelated to each other for the total sample, the two are inversely related among the Luo. Thus, among the Luo, the lower the level of powerlessness, the more likely that individuals will be estranged from politics. Individuals who see no possibility of changing their environment are also those who are most likely to show lower levels of political estrangement, while those with the strongest feelings

Table 5.10. Powerlessness by Perception of Improvement in Living Standards in the City and on a Personal Level since Independence, Tribalism Items, and Estrangement by Tribe

	Total Sample	Kikuyu	Luo
Living conditions in city improved?	.05 (498)	−.03 (179)	−.15 (114)
Living conditions—personal—improved?	.05 (498)	.03 (179)	.08 (114)
How serious the problem of government officials doing special favors for their close friends and relatives?	.06 (497)	.01 (179)	.11 (114)
Are politicians stirring up tribal differences or trying to eliminate tribalism?	.11* (498)	.13 (179)	−.01 (114)
How serious a problem is tribalism in Nairobi?	.06 (498)	.13 (179)	.06 (114)
Estrangement	−.04 (498)	.03 (179)	−.19† (114)

* Significant at the .01 level.
† Significant at the .05 level.
Sample sizes in parentheses.

of political efficacy are most estranged. No relationship between the two exists among the Kikuyu, indicating differential opportunities to participate and differential social support for political attitudes. The lack of any relationship between powerlessness and other political attitudes suggests that it is perhaps a more general belief which is less related to recent political events than other attitudes. For example, despite the strong differences between the Kikuyu and Luo on most political attitudes, the distribution of powerlessness scores for the two groups is virtually the same.

Conclusions

Ethnicity, life-style, and social status are all related to political attitudes in Nairobi in different ways. Positive and negative feelings about the government and politicians are most clearly associated with ethnic group membership. In addition, ethnicity shapes the way in which life-style and social status are related to political beliefs within different tribal groups. One question to pursue is the way in which these attitudes are associated with political participation, but before considering this problem we first turn to a discussion of political participation in Nairobi.

Chapter 6 Political Participation and Increasing Scale—I

Political participation in any society can be viewed as a function both of individuals' dispositions and resources and of the participation opportunities open to them. As with political attitudes, our interest in political involvement is in patterns of variation in Nairobi. As a first step toward explanation, we offer several hypotheses linking political activity to life-style and social status through comparisons of individuals in terms of the scale of their social relations.

African participation in Kenyan national politics, as opposed to local authority systems, is historically quite recent. In a country where face-to-face patterns of political communication are in the process of being replaced by more indirect and representative institutions, one important question is about what kinds of individuals are likely to be highly active in the new system. On the one hand, certain people might be expected to be active politically irrespective of the dominant form which participation takes. Conversely, different forms of political activity may recruit individuals on the basis of particular skills and motivations. These competing hypotheses raise a question about the extent to which historical and social conditions are likely to be associated with a change in the basis of recruitment into political activity.

Answering this question requires examination of the mechanisms of political recruitment. The theory of increasing scale suggests that patterns of participation are a function of societal scale.[1] Scale is the extent of interdependence, both material and normative, linking individuals and communities. Differences in participation patterns can be identified both across societies varying in scale position and within a single society where the scale positions of individuals or groups are indicated by the range and intensity of their social relations.[2] One way to analyze how differences in political and social participation in contemporary Africa are a function of social structural conditions, therefore, is to distinguish between individuals or groups having high and low scale positions.

Employing the concept of the *scale of social relations* to compare individuals, one can attempt to understand different bases of political recruitment. Within a single community or city, individuals show great variation in the scale of their social relations; consequently they have differential access to political and social institutions. Some individuals have a wide range of social contacts, know a large number of people, and travel a great deal within the community. Others do not leave their neighborhoods very often, have only a few friends, and are much more home oriented. Furthermore, in African cities such as Nairobi, where a large percentage of the wives and children of urban residents spend a sizable proportion of their time living in the rural areas, and where contact between the rural areas and the city is extremely high, many urban residents can be described as oriented as much to rural life as to life in the city.

If political activity attracts the same types of individuals irrespective of its particular forms, we would hypothesize that individuals with the widest range of social relations would exhibit the highest levels of political participation. Because politics is essentially a secondary activity, it is expected that individuals with the widest range of social interactions are most likely to have more extensive ties and greater experience in the kinds of associations relevant for political action. Individuals with a wide range of social ties are likely to have the highest access to participation structures. Thus, if one or two possible channels for participation are blocked or inoperative, an individual with a relatively wide range of associations can turn to alternative channels that would not be available to the persons with a more limited set of social relations.

If different forms of political activity recruit different types of people, those with a high scale position should be most likely to be involved in activities that are best promoted through extensive and diverse social ties, while those with low scale positions should be most likely to be involved in activities that are developed through intensive but more limited social contacts. The way in which an individual's scale position is related to participation varies with the extent to which he develops mechanisms of participation on his own as opposed to the extent to which he is in a highly organized community that provides participation opportunities to those people most involved in local social relations. Thus, when local political organizations are strong, people with the most intensive and limited ties (low scale positions) should be most active, particularly in party and electoral politics, whereas when participation is more individualistic and less organized, those with more extensive and diverse contacts (high scale position) and greater personal resources should be most involved.[3]

Measures of Political Participation and the Scale of Social Relations
Political participation refers to the behaviors of individuals designed to affect either directly or indirectly the outcomes of political decisions.[4] An individual who works for a political party during an election campaign or a person who visits a public official's office is directly participating in politics. Others participate more indirectly by following political news in the press or radio and engaging in political discussions with their friends and family. In addition, by participating an individual does not necessarily accept or approve of existing political institutions or leaders, and it should be realized that often participation is aimed at changing or overthrowing either or both.

In order to measure political participation each respondent was asked:

Now I am going to read to you a list of some of the ways in which people participate in politics. After I read each way people participate, please tell me whether you do these things these days.
  (1) Follow the news about politics on the radio
  (2) Follow the news about politics in the newspapers
  (3) Talk about politics with friends
  (4) Talk about politics with family and relatives
  (5) Attend political rallies or meetings
Now I will read some more ways in which people can participate and I would like you to tell me if you have *ever* done any of these things.
  (6) Vote
  (7) Join a political party
  (8) Pay dues to a political party
  (9) Write a letter to a newspaper
 (10) Write a letter to your MP
 (11) Write a letter to your city councillor
 (12) Visit a session of parliament
 (13) Attend a city council meeting
 (14) Work for a candidate to get him elected
 (15) Go and see a government official when you had a problem
 (16) Have you ever met the MP from this constituency personally?
 (17) Have you ever met your city councillor personally?
 (18) Are you at present registered on the new Electoral Roll (1967)?

Initially we intended to use all of these items to compute a political participation index for each respondent. Before doing this, however, it was necessary to test for "single factoredness," that is, to determine whether or not the 18 items actually represented a single dimension that could be called political activity or political participation. Therefore, all of the items were factor analyzed and the unrotated solution examined.[5] The results showed that participation was clearly not unidimensional; however, the unrotated solution was not useful in distinguishing between the several dimensions. Table 6.1 presents the rotated solution, which shows that indeed the 18 items comprise two independent dimensions.[6]

The two dimensions show two forms of mass political participation

Table 6.1. Factor Loading of Political Participation Items. Rotated Solution*

Variable	Factor 1	Factor 2	Communality
1. Radio	(.522)	.083	.279
2. Newspapers	(.527)	−.041	.279
3. Talk with Friends	(.599)	.051	.361
4. Talk with Family	(.525)	.048	.278
5. Attend Meetings	.271	(.392)	.227
6. Vote	−.013	(.582)	.338
7. Join a Party	.063	(.750)	.566
8. Pay Party Dues	.168	(.708)	.530
9. Write to a Newspaper	(.399)	.117	.173
10. Write to MP	(.388)	.224	.200
11. Write Councillor	(.292)	.185	.119
12. Visit Parliament	(.464)	.025	.216
13. Visit Council	(.292)	.271	.159
14. Help a Candidate	.201	(.447)	.240
15. Go to a Government Office	(.476)	.193	.264
16. Meet MP	.229	.223	.102
17. Meet Councillor	.181	.250	.096
18. Register to Vote	−.072	(.480)	.236
Sum of Squares over Variables	2.342	2.322	

* An individual's score on each of these dimensions is based on an index compiled from each of the items with at least a .290 loading on that factor. Thus, the independence-style dimension, Factor 2, is based on items 5, 6, 7, 8, 14, and 18, while the postindependence participation score, Factor 1, is based on items 1, 2, 3, 4, 9, 10, 11, 12, 13, and 15. Factor scores for individuals were not used because of missing data.

in Nairobi, which reflect changes from the independence to the post-independence eras. Factor 2 contains those aspects of participation that are most closely associated with political participation during the independence period. Each of the items—attendance at rallies or meetings, voting, joining a party, paying party dues, working for a candidate to get him elected, and registering to vote—are related to party or electoral activity, the two areas of political activity that were most important during the independence period. People can still participate in these activities today. The question about registration, for example, concerned a new list of registered voters that was compiled while the research was conducted.

Factor 1 reflects the style of participation that has grown more important since independence. It is unrelated to political party or electoral activity. The items on this dimension—following the news about politics on the radio, in the newspapers, talking about politics with friends, with family or relatives, writing letters to a newspaper, an MP, or a city councillor, attending a session of parliament or the city council, and going to see a government official about a problem—reflect two aspects of the postindependence political style: (1) the obtaining of political information through the media or social contacts, and (2) the development of channels to communicate with political or administrative officials. In summary, *the independence style reflects the response of the population to the mobilization efforts of the political elite,* while *the postindependence style shows a pattern of activity in which the population seeks to acquire information and present its views and demands to the elite.*

Explaining Differences in Participation Levels

The three dimensions of urban social structure, ethnicity, social status, and life-style, offer a starting point for explanation of differences in levels of political participation on each of our two independent dimensions of activity. This should permit us to understand how each form of political involvement recruits different types of individuals, as well as to characterize the types of people most drawn to each form of activity on the basis of participation opportunities and individual resources.

ETHNICITY

Although group membership is an excellent predictor of political attitudes in Nairobi, it has no relationship to *level* of political activity. At least in the city, political involvement in either style of participation is not a function of an individual's ethnicity.[7] This does not necessarily mean, however, that political activities and organizations are multi-tribal, as it certainly is possible that participation continues on an intratribal basis, with most participation, particularly in the post-independence style, occurring within small ethnically homogeneous groups.

SOCIAL STATUS AND THE SCALE OF SOCIAL RELATIONS

Political participation is not unidimensional, and therefore it is necessary to specify the ways in which *each* participation style might be related to an individual's scale of social relations. The political independence movement in Kenya can be considered a mass move-ment. Led by the Kenya African National Union (KANU), the move-ment mobilized large numbers of people to participate in national level politics for the first time. Such mass movements most frequently recruit members from the most alienated, the most disadvantaged groups in society.[8] Since attaining independence in 1963, the political party and other structures aimed at mobilizing political participation have been relatively unimportant. The leaders of the independence movement are now a governing elite and are no longer interested in encouraging wide-scale political activity that they consider dysfunc-tional to economic development and threatening to their own posi-tions. Therefore, we expect that *social status will be negatively related to the independence style participation and positively related to the postindependence style.* Individuals with the lowest levels of education and with the lowest incomes are likely to have been the most active during the independence struggle, while in the postindependence period, in the absence of a mass movement that permits and encour-ages widespread political participation, special skills associated with education and income are likely to be necessary for effective participa-tion in politics. Similarly, Austin suggests in his discussion of the Convention People's Party during the independence period in Ghana that the "Standard Seven boys" (those people who left school after completing their primary education) provided the basis of Nkrumah's support. These people were unable to find the jobs their education led them to expect and were most dissatisfied with their situation under the colonial government. The CPP took advantage of the situation and mobilized them into political activity during the 1950s.

It was from this broad social group of elementary-school-leavers that the leaders of the radical wing of the nationalist movement were drawn in 1949. . . . And the CPP was to win its first election victory in 1951 over the earlier generation of political leaders, not merely because it outbid UGCC in terms of 'Self-Government Now' rather than 'later', but because it enlisted in its ranks the general body of commoners-literate and illiterate alike.[9]

Participation in the postindependence pattern, on the other hand, often requires certain special skills. Literacy is helpful, although not essential, to follow the news about politics in the papers or for writing to government officials. It is also useful in dealing with and understanding the workings of the bureaucracy. Social status may also be important in that many Africans still feel a great gap between themselves and government officials, something which many African bureaucrats have taken advantage of in the same way as their colonial predecessors. In Kenya, for example, an African who enters a government office without a tie or clean suit or without being able to conduct his business in English is often quickly made to feel inferior.

The opposite effects of social status upon the two participation styles are seen clearly in Table 6.2. As suggested in the mass society theory,

Table 6.2. Political Participation Styles by Education Level, Income Group, Male, Length of Residence in Nairobi, Percent of Life in Nairobi since Age 15, and Contact with the Rural Areas

	Independence Style	Postindependence Style
Education Level	−.29* (492)	.32* (492)
Income Group	−.12* (484)	.19* (484)
Male	.22* (498)	.29* (498)
Length of Residence in Nairobi	.35* (496)	−.05 (496)
Percent of Life in Nairobi since Age 15	.15* (496)	.06 (496)
Contact with the Rural Areas	−.06 (491)	.15* (498)

* Significant at the .01 level.
Sample sizes in parentheses.

individuals with the most disadvantaged positions in society are most likely to participate in mass movements such as the independence political movement, while individuals with higher social status are most likely to participate in politics in the absence of these movements. The data show that education and income are negatively related to the independence style while they are positively related to the post-independence style of political participation.[10]

LIFE-STYLE AND THE SCALE OF SOCIAL RELATIONS
Life-style differences in Nairobi are the different social choices that individuals make about the organization of their lives in the city. Specifically, there are differences between men and women, differences in the degree of contact with the rural areas, and differences in the kinds of social networks in the city in which one is involved. Each of these should be related to the two styles of political participation.
Sex. Social differences between men and women in Nairobi are striking. A woman in the city is viewed more negatively than a man. Furthermore, women generally operate in a more limited social network than men, in the sense that they are likely to have a smaller range of interactions than men, come in contact with a smaller number of people during the course of a day, and stay in the city for shorter periods of time. All of this suggests that they are less likely to be mobilized into the political action than men, and, in fact, whether we refer to the independence or postindependence styles of political participation, we expect that *men will be more politically active than women.*

This is supported in the data presented in Table 6.2, which shows that the only similarity between the two participation styles is that men are more politically active than women. One possible explanation is that the differences between the sexes in the postindependence style are a function of men's higher education, longer length of residence in the city, or older age. However, if the partial correlations are computed for each of these three variables, the correlations between sex and both participation styles are still significant.
City residence. Relatively long term residence in the city should be positively related to participation in those situations where individuals are mobilized to participate through their social networks. This should

be especially important in recruiting individuals into the independence movement, where mobilization into political activity should be a functon of the range and depth of an individual's social contacts. A person who has lived in the city for a long time and who has spent a large percentage of his life in the city is likely to have more extensive social contacts and therefore is also more likely than a recent migrant to the city to participate in the independence-style politics. On the other hand, political participation that is less dependent upon specific membership groups, and less formalized, such as the postindependence participation style should be more independent of the range of an individual's social network. Therefore, *length of residence in the city and the percentage of life than an individual spends in the city should be more related to the independence participation style than to the postindependence style.*

This hypothesis is also confirmed by the data in Table 6.2, which shows that both length of residence in the city and the percentage of life that an individual has spent in the city since age 15 are positively related to the independence participation style, while neither is related to postindependence participation. This suggests that the face-to-face interactions of city life and the extent of social orientation to the city were more important in drawing individuals into the independence movement than in developing political participants today. Apparently the basis of recruitment has shifted.

Contact with rural areas. A second way to evaluate an individual's social networks is to consider the degree of contact he maintains with rural areas. Our hypothesis suggests that contact with the rural areas should be positively related to political participation because individuals who maintain higher contact will have a wider range of social ties that can be politicized.

Austin's[11] observations on the basis of the independence movement in Ghana suggest that participation in the independence style should be negatively related to contact with the rural areas. Individuals most active in party and electoral activity should be those without rural alternatives. Sklar and Whitaker, on the other hand, contend that political participation in Nigeria is really participation on the basis of communal affinity to ethnic or religous groups. They define "party alignment on a Gemeinschaft or communal basis. . . . . . (as one in which) members and supporters conceive of their party as an extension of a social order into which they have been born and to which they attribute spiritual or mystical significance."[12] Gesellschaft, or associational participation, which they define as "purposeful alignment on the basis of a perceived interest," is found most frequently in the urban areas.

The data in Table 6.2 show that contact with the rural areas is positively related to the postindependence participation style, as Sklar and Whitaker suggest; however, it is generally unrelated to the independence style. As far as the postindependence style is concerned, then, range of social relations as measured by contact with the rural areas is positively related to participation as predicted, a finding which is consistent with our more general proposition that individuals with the greatest range of associations are likely to be the most active politically.

Friendship patterns. Maintenance of contact with the rural areas is one source of the wide social networks that are related to participation in politics. Another is the development of friendship networks in the city which extend outside the individual's neighborhood and which include people whom he first met in Nairobi and who are not from his birthplace or tribe. Two contradictory hypotheses regarding the nature of the relationship between friendship networks in the city and political participation are both reasonable. The first is that the more insular pattern, wherein a greater proportion of a person's friends are in his own neighborhood, from his own birthplace or tribe, and from home rather than the city, will be related to greater activity in politics. This would mean that people use localized, ethnic friendship networks for the transmission of political information and for carrying on political activity. If politics in the city is basically communal in nature, in the manner in which Sklar and Whitaker define the term, then we would expect individuals who are most involved in localized, ethnically oriented networks to be most active politically. The alternative hypothesis, already presented, is that participation in politics is promoted through the contacts individuals have outside their communal groups, and that individuals who operate in broader friendship networks, outside their neighborhood and ethnic group, are in a better position to obtain information and to interact with politicians or administrators. The broader range of interaction provides them with greater information about the operation of the political processes in the city and makes them better able to participate in politics.

The data in Table 6.3 support the second hypothesis. Having close friends outside one's neighborhood of residence, place of birth, and tribe, and having friends made in Nairobi rather than at home are positively associated with the postindependence participation style although there is no relationship between friendship patterns and the independence style of political participation.

These data from Nairobi show two distinct forms of mass political participation and demonstrate that different types of people are likely to be recruited into each. Individuals who are high in the scale of social relations, or people of high social status, men, long-term city residents, people maintaining high contact with the rural areas, and individuals with the most diverse friendship networks are likely to be relatively high on the postindependence style. Possessing greater individual resources, these people are more capable, and possibly more motivated, to develop and maintain individualistic participation mechanisms. In contrast, the data present a less clear case concerning

Table 6.3. Participation Styles by Urban Friendship Patterns

	Independence Style	Postindependence Style
(1)	.05 (474)	−.13* (474)
(2)	.00 (469)	−.16* (469)
(3)	−.01 (451)	−.10† (451)
(4)	.02 (475)	−.14* (475)
(5)	.02 (472)	−.19* (472)
(6)	.01 (462)	−.10† (462)
(7)	.06 (477)	.10† (477)

* Significant at the .01 level.
† Significant at the .05 level.
Sample sizes in parentheses.
(1) First friend from estate of residence.
(2) First friend from same district of birth.
(3) First friend from same tribe.
(4) Percent of friends from same estate.
(5) Percent of friends from same birthplace.
(6) Percent of friends from same tribe.
(7) Percent of friends made in Nairobi.

individuals who are low on the scale of social relations. There is partial support for the interpretation that such individuals with more limited and intensive social ties are those who are most likely to participate in party and electoral politics, and are most active when strong organizations, such as a political machine, draw them into politics.

Conclusion

Two distinct styles of political participation in Nairobi are identifiable, the independence style which reflects the mobilization efforts of the political elite and the postindependence pattern which shows efforts of the population to acquire political information and present their views to the elite. Recruitment into each form of activity is very different, as participation in the independence style is greatest among the most disadvantaged groups in the city, while postindependence participation draws individuals from the highest status categories.

In considering the relationship between ethnicity, social class, lifestyle, and participation, the data generally show stronger correlations between the elements of social organization and postindependence participation than between these elements and the independence style. For example, contact with the rural areas and the heterogeneity of social networks in Nairobi are related to postindependence participation but not to the independence style. The range and diversity of an individual's social networks are much better predictors of his level of involvement on the postindependence dimension. This suggests that the two participation styles are themselves indicators of the changing scale of Kenyan society. Previous studies by Clignet and Sween and McElrath have shown that the higher the scale position of a society, the more clearly the process of social differentiation is marked. In this case, the postindependence style may be seen as a marker of increasing social and political differentiation in Nairobi.[13]

Chapter 7 Political Participation and Increasing Scale—II

Participation in politics can be direct or indirect. Some activities are themselves overtly political, while others may dispose people toward political action at future times. This chapter considers two activities of the latter sort: the possession of knowledge and information about the actors in the political game, and membership in formal groups. Each of these should dispose people toward political activity for a different reason. Information about politics provides individuals with knowledge that can be useful in being skillful participants, that is, in trying to produce favorable outcomes on specific issues. Formal group membership should be relevant because it may provide individuals with structures through which their involvement can be channeled.

Political Information and Participation

Studies elsewhere have found a positive relationship between political knowledge and participation as well as between political knowledge and such socioeconomic indicators as education and income.[1] However, if political knowledge is positively related to participation in Nairobi, it is first necessary to ask to which style of participation it should be related. On the one hand, it might be argued that the politicians in Kenya are the contemporary Kenyan "folk-heroes." Politics is highly personalized in most areas of Africa, and it might be hypothesized that the people most involved in the most personalized area—electoral and party politics, the trademarks of independence-style participation —should have the greatest knowledge of the political actors. The alternative hypothesis is that independence politics socialized people to a more general set of symbols, the most prominent of which was *uhuru* (independence), and to personalized awareness of only the most prominent of the political figures, such as Kenyatta, Mboya, or Odinga. Therefore, individuals who participate in the postindependence style should possess greater knowledge about the political actors, for they receive a greater stream of information about politics on a day-to-day basis and this information is reinforced more frequently. The data in Table 7.1 support this second hypothesis. It shows that the correlations between all four political information items—being able to name the MP, the city councillor, the recently appointed

Table 7.1. Political Information Items by Participation Styles

	Independence Style	Postindependence Style
Name Member of Parliament	.15* (486)	.17* (486)
Name City Councillor	.08 (483)	.10† (483)
Name Minister for East African Affairs	.05 (493)	.26* (493)
Number of Ministers Named Correctly	.00 (497)	.30* (497)

* Significant at the .01 level.
† Significant at the .05 level.
Sample sizes are in parentheses.

minister for East African Affairs, and the number of members of the cabinet—is positively related to the postindependence political style, while only one—knowledge of one's MP—was significantly related to the independence political style.[2]

Formal Group Membership and Political Participation
Voluntary associations are often an important adaptive mechanism by which migrants in African cities cope with the complexities of urban life:

. . . . the migrant's participation in some organization such as tribal union or a dancing *compin* not only replaces much of what he has lost in terms of moral assurance in removing from his native village, but offers him companionship and an opportunity of sharing joys as well as sorrows with others in the same position as himself.[3]

Little distinguishes between three different types of voluntary associations: (1) those concerned with traditional activities, although with some slight modification; (2) those in which traditional activities have been deliberately modified or expanded to suit modern purposes; and (3) those that are wholly modern in organization and objectives.[4] What is common to all of these organizations is the function of providing the migrant with companions who can provide social support for recreation and mutual aid. Little asserts that in West Africa the members of voluntary associations are generally young people, and that they establish new criteria for achievement in the towns, particularly for women and those in the younger age groups.[5]

In East Africa, and more particularly in Nairobi, voluntary associations do not appear to be as prominent as the literature on West

African cities suggests they are on the other side of the continent. Perhaps this is because length of residence in Nairobi is generally shorter than in most West African cities, or perhaps it is due to the greater domination of the Europeans and Asians in the economy, which would have inhibited the growth of such organizations as African traders associations. While there are probably fewer formally organized voluntary associations in Nairobi than in West African cities, there are many "informal" associations serving the same functions. Men, frequently from the same place of work and from the same location in the rural areas, get together, for example, and contribute Shs. 50/– or 100/–, which is then placed in a bank account which members can draw upon in times of need.

Table 7.2 gives the characteristics of individuals who are most likely to be members of voluntary associations.[6] Men have a greater tendency to join associations than women. Members of formal organizations in Nairobi are likely to be older, to have lived in the city longer and a greater percentage of their lives, to have a greater intensity of contact with the rural areas, to have a greater percentage of friends from outside their estate, and a greater percentage of friends met in the city rather than at home.[7]

Membership in voluntary associations is one mechanism for moving the migrant in the city into broader social networks and an expanded

Table 7.2. Formal Group Membership by Sex, Age, Length of Residence in the City, Percent of Life Spent in the City, Percent of Life in City since 15, Contact with the Rural Areas, Number of Acres of Land Owned in the Rural Areas, Percent of Friends from Respondent's Estate, and Percent of Friends Met in the City

	Correlation	Sample Size
Male	.25*	(498)
Age	.18*	(498)
Length of Residence	.21*	(496)
Percent Life in City	.19*	(496)
Percent Life in City since 15	.15*	(496)
Contact with the Rural Areas Index	.13*	(498)
Number of Acres of Land	.10†	(494)
Percent Friends from Respondent's Estate	−.09†	(475)
Percent Friends from City	.09†	(477)

* Significant at .01 level.
† Significant at .05 level.

range of social activities. Political activity can serve the same function. Therefore, it is possible to hypothesize two different relationships between political participation and formal group membership. On the one hand, membership in formal groups or participation in politics may move the individual into broader social networks which have a "spillover effect" so that people drawn into participation in one sphere, such as voluntary associations, are drawn also into participation in politics. Voluntary associations, then, even if explicitly nonpolitical, can serve to draw people into political activity. The alternative hypothesis is that individuals gain companionship either from participation in certain voluntary associations or from participation in politics, and therefore people who participate in one activity are less likely to engage in the other.

Table 7.3 presents the relationship between voluntary group membership and the two styles of political participation. It shows clearly that voluntary group membership is highly correlated with *both* styles of political activity. The data also indicate that there are differences between the style of political participation and *which* voluntary associations an individual is a member of, except for church membership, which is not related to either participation style.

The data in Table 7.3 support the hypothesis that there is a spillover effect between political activity and voluntary group membership. It is impossible, of course, from these data to suggest any directional effect

Table 7.3. Participation Style by Formal Group Membership

	Independence Style	Postindependence Style
Formal Group Index	.49* (498)	.34* (498)
Union	.36* (491)	.18* (491)
Welfare, District, or Tribal Association	.22* (492)	.21* (492)
Church	−.05 (489)	.05 (489)
Political Party	.56* (490)	.14* (490)
Sports Club	.09† (491)	.27* (491)
Other Group	.08 (462)	.14* (462)

* Significant at the .01 level.
† Significant at the .05 level.
Sample sizes in parentheses.

between the two forms of activity. But participation in certain
kinds of voluntary associations is more highly related to certain styles
of political activity. Union membership, for example, is much more
highly related to the independence style than to the postindependence
style, which confirms the notion of a number of authors who have
suggested that during the independence period in Africa the trade-
union movements were often mobilized in support of the independence
movement. Membership in a welfare, district, or tribal association is
associated with both styles of participation at the same level, while
membership in either a sports club, such as a football association, or
other formal group is more highly related to the postindependence
style. These groups, which are far less likely to be brought directly
into party and electoral activity, do attract individuals who engage in
activities relating to the acquisition of political information and communication with the administration and politicians.

Sex Differences in Participation[8]
Urbanization is a very different experience for men and women in
Nairobi at present, as we argued in Chapter 3. Attitudes about living
in the city and opportunities for social participation differ for the two
sexes. One consequence is that the overall level of political participation is much higher for men than for women in both the independence
and postindependence styles, as reported in Chapter 6. In addition to
finding that the level of political activity is a function of sex, we now
present data showing that *within* each sex group, political involvement
is explained by somewhat different variables associated with the different meaning of city life for men and women in Nairobi.

Social status is associated with both male and female political participation in a more uniform way than life-style. In general, education, income, and occupational status are negatively associated with
independence participation and positively related to postindependence
participation, for both sexes. There are important differences between
men and women, however, when we consider the effects of two life-
style choices, contact with the rural areas and friendship patterns in
the city.

The higher the level of independence-style participation, the higher
the level of contact with the rural areas for men, while among women

the pattern is just the opposite. Women with the weakest ties to home are the most involved in electoral and party politics in Nairobi, possibly because high involvement in both domains at the same time is not open to them as it is for a man. Looking at postindependence participation, however, these differences disappear as involvement increases with contact with the rural areas for both sexes. Perhaps this means that there are fewer normative restrictions on women's political involvement when it does not involve public activity, or possibly this is more a reflection of the fact that postindependence participation is related to education and income, and that the effects of social status cut across sex lines.[9]

While friendship patterns are not associated with the independence style, they are related, in different ways for each sex, to postindependence involvement.[10] The higher the proportion of his friends an individual has from outside his estate, from outside his tribe and district of birth, and the more friends he met in the city, the greater the level of his postindependence participation. For men, having friends from outside their district of birth as well as friends whom they met in the city is most significant, while for women having their closest friend from outside their own estate, friends from outside their own estate, and friends from outside their tribe and birthplace are situations associated with higher participation.

Formal group membership is another way to view an individual's range of social interaction in the city. Men are more likely to be members of voluntary associations than women. However, the importance of this difference between the sexes varies with the type of association. Men are more often members of a labor union, a welfare, district or tribal association, or sports club, while women are more likely to be members of a church congregation. For both men and women, membership in formal groups is associated with their length of residence in the city and with the proportion of their life spent in the city. A high level of contact with the rural areas is associated with group membership for men, while females who are highly participatory have a lower proportion of friends from their tribe and a greater proportion whom they met in the city.

Political participation for men is associated more with the maintenance of ties to the rural areas, while for women participation is consistently more a function of a broader network of friendships within Nairobi. The different meaning of city life for men and women provides a partial explanation for the reasons why different life-style choices are related to political involvement for each sex group.

In many cases a woman comes to the city because social alternatives are closed to her in the rural area. She may be barren, or, on the other hand, she may find herself unmarriageable because she has had several illegitimate children; or after her husband's death, his remaining kin may have forced her to leave his land. Even if she has come to the city to live with her husband, she may have done so only after having a severe altercation with his family who want her to stay in the rural areas to work on his land. In any case, it is usually the man's role to maintain the contacts with the rural relatives and to travel home for funerals and other ritual occasions. At home politics is not considered to be her concern, at least until she is well into middle age. A woman, then, who increases her scale of social interaction is more likely to do this within the urban environment than through rural contacts. In the city she can develop friendships with people residing in other housing estates, who are members of other tribes, and who were born in districts other than her own. This is especially true if she is working or can afford to hire someone to care for her children part of the day, enabling her to move about in the city. For a man there is less conflict between his urban and rural roles insofar as he remains a participant in both communities. Men travel home more frequently and, in addition, their rural roles are more compatible with political activity and interest at an earlier age than they are for women. Extensive ties to the rural areas for men lead to politicization, while for women these ties apparently serve other purposes. In contrast, for women extensive ties within the city are more relevant to political involvement.

Conclusions

The forms of political participation in any society can show a good deal of variation. Our data suggest that each participation style is likely to be associated with different social groups and a different recruitment base for activists of each type. The concept of the scale of social relations is useful in explaining our findings because it permits us to distinguish individual level differences in the social change process. Postindependence participation, political information, and formal group memberships are all higher for individuals with relatively high scale positions—namely, those with higher social status, higher levels of contact with the rural area, and with heterogeneous and extensive friendship networks. Thus, the scale of social relations must include not only urban interaction patterns but consider the wider society in which an individual is located.

Both rural and urban Kenya are part of the same social system.[11] Goals that are established in one sector often determine behavior patterns in the other. For example, a man often uses his income from city employment to further rural goals, by buying land, cattle, or paying a bride-price. Movement out of the rural sphere of influence, then, does not mean that an individual has moved into a wider network of social relations. On the contrary, it may simply mean that he lacks the resources and abilities to maintain rural ties.

The scale of social relations varies across individuals so that some people operate in networks that are both limited and homogeneous, while others have social ties that are extended and diverse. The importance of variation in scale for politics is that individuals with the more limited and homogeneous networks had a greater chance of being mobilized during the struggle for political independence, while those with the extended and diverse ties are most active in the postindependence period. During the former period the elite mobilized large numbers to place political pressure on the colonial government. After independence this mobilization ended, and individuals have had to rely upon their own resources to be active in politics. Individuals with low-scale positions are likely to be active when they are part of highly organized communities which provide participation opportunities through these local structures. In contrast, people with high-scale positions are active when participation is dependent upon participation opportunities which are more individually based and require greater skill in manipulating the social environment.

Chapter 8   Political Participation and Alienation

While the concepts of political participation and political alienation are central to much of modern political analysis, the relationship between them is not well understood. In Nairobi, our evidence shows that both take several forms, and that the social basis of each behavior or belief varies considerably. We turn now to a consideration of how participation and alienation are related to each other.

The most frequently encountered hypothesis is that political alienation and participation are inversely related. The alienated, this argument runs, are likely to have little interest in politics, and consequently, their active involvement is low. At the same time, there are other analyses that focus on precisely the opposite hypothesis, looking for political conditions and movements that mobilize the most alienated and disaffected elements of society.

One source of the confusion is the assumption that political alienation[1] is a unidimensional concept, an unwarranted assumption whether one considers studies, such as this one, that find low or no correlations between different dimensions of alienation,[2] or takes account of the different social structural conditions associated with different dimensions of political alienation. In general, political powerlessness is much more highly related, in a negative direction, to participation than are other dimensions of alienation, such as estrangement. In both political and nonpolitical settings there is widespread support for the proposition that an individual's sense of efficacy is directly related to his behavioral involvement.[3]

The relationship between political participation and other forms of alienation is a good deal less clear. Unlike the powerless, individuals manifesting other forms of political alienation do not necessarily reject the idea of meaningful political action. For example, Aberbach finds that while powerlessness[4] is related to voting turnout in the United States, it is not significantly related to the direcion of the vote. Political trust, on the other hand, is unrelated to turnout or political participation, but is correlated with partisanship and the direction of the vote.[5] Similarly Finifter reports powerlessness to be much more highly related to participation than perceived political normlessness is, and in a multiple regression she finds the regression coefficient between participation and normlessness is positive, although small.[6]

The spillover from one dimension of alienation to another is often weak; an individual's position on one dimension tells little or nothing about his score on others. Finifter therefore suggests that characteristic forms of participation may be associated with the interrelationship of different dimensions of alienation. Taking powerlessness and perceived political normlessness, she presents a 2 by 2 table showing different forms of participation associated with each combination. High powerlessness and high normlessness result in extreme disengagement from a political system, either in the form of complete withdrawal from politics or participation in separatist organizations or mass movements, while high normlessness and low powerlessness result in a reform orientation characterized by protest activity within an existing institutional framework.[7] Keniston also shows that the politically estranged are not necessarily powerless. In fact estrangement may derive from the belief that meaningful political action to change social conditions is indeed possible but is being thwarted by particular politicians or political institutions.[8] It seems that estranged individuals are likely to be politically active when participation opportunities are available which allow them to express their attitudinal orientations.[9] Mass society theorists discuss some of these situations in which highly alienated individuals are likely to participate in politics.[10] These theorists are particularly interested in the social conditions that give rise to mass movements, extremist political organizations, and authoritarian regimes. Alienation is a crucial intervening variable in their formulations. It results from social conditions, such as rapid urbanization, industrialization, and severe social dislocation, which separate individuals from well-defined positions in the social structure, making them susceptible to mobilization into mass movements.[11] Mass movements mobilize people who are alienated from the going system, who do not believe in the legitimacy of the established order, and who therefore are ready to engage in efforts to destroy it. The greatest number of people available to mass movements will be found in those sections of society that have the fewest ties to the social order, for those who have the fewest opportunities to participate have the weakest commitments to existing institutions.[12]

In addition to participation opportunities, political participation for both the alienated and nonalienated is likely to be dependent on the social support an individual receives from primary and peer groups. Recruitment into highly activist political roles shows the still strong influence of primary group and kinship ties in a modern industrial society such as the United States.[13] Even in supposedly mass-based political organizations, there is strong evidence that recruitment and continued participation are much more dependent upon face-to-face direct contacts with peers than on particular ideology or the presence of a charismatic leader on the national level.[14] The Asch experiments in a laboratory setting show that, while support for an individual does not have to be near unanimous or even represent a majority, its complete absence is highly related to individuals' conformity to group attitudes.[15] The presence or absence of social support would then appear to be crucial in understanding the dynamics of participation, particularly in cases where individuals are likely to advocate unpopular views and actions or those that violate widely held norms or beliefs.

In understanding how a person's attitudes are related to his political behaviors, it is important to consider social structural factors as intervening variables that create differential participation opportunities and social support. Therefore, feelings of estrangement are most likely to be positively associated with participation when social structural conditions create participation opportunities and social support consistent with these attitudes, and negatively when these conditions are absent.

In considering the relationship between social structure and political attitudes toward the government in Chapter 5, we suggested ways in which Kikuyus and Luos are likely to develop different political attitudes. Ethnic group membership, in effect, represents different patterns of social support for particular attitudes and different participation opportunities for their expression. Therefore, considering our previous findings we suggest the following hypotheses:

1. Both independence and postindependence participation will be negatively related to feelings of powerlessness among both the Kikuyu and Luo.

2. Both independence and postindependence participation will be
   positively related to estrangement among the Luo and negatively
   related to estrangement among the Kikuyu.

The first hypothesis argues that the stronger the feelings of powerlessness, the less likely an individual will participate in politics, refer-
ring both to party and electoral activity associated with the independence style and to the less-public and organized forms of political
activity associated with the postindependence style. Political participation requires an investment in time and energy, and individuals who
strongly believe that there is little that can be done to affect political
decision making in their society are not very likely to make this investment. There should be no difference whether we refer to the independence or postindependence participation styles because in both
situations the individuals is likely to come to the same conclusion.

The second hypothesis relating estrangement and participation is
more complicated because of the introduction of tribe as an intervening variable. Because of the nature of the data, we are attempting to
relate participation in party and electoral activity, primarily associated
with the independence period, to feeling toward the government in
the postindependence era; however, we are not considering attitudes
toward the colonial government as they related to attempts to over-
throw it. Individuals who participate in an activity later tend to view
that activity more favorably than individuals who are not active.
Participants do not want to think that their efforts were in vain. Therefore, it should be expected that the more time and energy that an
individual invested in participating in the independence movement,
the more favorably he would come to see the government, which
symbolizes his successful efforts, at a later point in time.

On the other hand, there are often people who are very active in a
political or social movement who later break with the movement and
violently condemn its leaders, attacking them for abusing their positions and subordinating the movement's original goals. Examples of
this are the dispute between the Russian and Chinese communists, the
conflict between Malcolm X and the Black Muslims after he left the
movement, or factionalism within some African political parties after
independence. In each of these cases, the people who originally were
active participants in the movement do not suggest that their original

participation was foolish; rather they argue that a group of leaders betrayed the followers by not keeping their promises. Trotsky, for example, did not doubt the necessity for the 1917 Revolution; he questioned Stalin's use of power in the late 1920s and 1930s. Because the high participants in a movement have a high psychological invest- ment, they are most likely to have the strongest negative feelings toward the leaders who betrayed them, if and when they become disillusioned.

In short, the most active participants should have the strongest feelings. Whether these feelings are negative or positive is determined by situational factors. In Kenya, the most important situational factor since independence has been tribe or ethnicity. Increasingly, the gov- ernment has come to be identified in the public's view with the Kikuyus, while the Luos dominate the opposition. Feelings of political estrangement today differ widely by tribe, with the Kikuyus more favorably oriented to the government than the Luo. Therefore, we hypothesize that Kikuyus who were most active in the independence movement will tend to be most favorably disposed toward the govern- ment today, while the Luos who are most opposed to the government and most estranged will be those who were most active in the inde- pendence movement. Thus, within each ethnic group, the pattern will be different, although in both groups, the more active in politics an individual is, the more likely he will hold the dominant views of his group. The same reasoning lies behind the second part of the hypoth- esis, which is that feelings of estrangement will be positively associ- ated with postindependence participation among the Luo and negatively associated with it among the Kikuyu.

These two hypotheses yield eight separate predictions if we analyze the data by participation style, by form of alienation, and by tribe. The correlation matrix presented in Table 8.1 shows that, while only four of the eight relationships are statistically significant, all eight are in the predicted direction. This is tentative support for the hypotheses.

Looking more carefully at the table suggests the following con- clusions:

As feelings of powerlessness increase, the level of political participa- tion decreases, at least for the postindependence style, for both ethnic groups and the total sample. This suggests that Kenyan politics is

Table 8.1. Political Participation Styles by Powerlessness and Estrangement by Tribe

| | Independence-Style Participation | | |
	Total	Kikuyu	Luo
Powerlessness	−.07 (498)	−.14† (179)	−.09 (114)
Estrangement	.04 (498)	−.07 (179)	.14 (114)

| | Postindependence-Style Participation | | |
	Total	Kikuyu	Luo
Powerlessness	−.18* (498)	−.24* (179)	−.18† (114)
Estrangement	.11* (498)	.02 (179)	.21† (114)

* Significant at the .01 level.
† Significant at the .05 level.
Sample sizes in parentheses.

becoming more bureaucratic and similar to politics in western countries where participation is often dependent upon the mastery of certain skills, such as literacy, an understanding of the bureaucracy, and where resources such as social status and wealth are important in distinguishing the active from the uninvolved. Powerlessness in Nairobi, as in other countries, is negatively related to education, income, and rural landownership.

As estrangement increases, postindependence participation increases among the total sample and Luo, while estrangement is unrelated to independence participation for all groups. As we have argued, among the Luo, and possibly among other groups as well, social support and participation opportunities are present that permit the estranged to become politically active. Through contact with the rural areas, as well as interactions with fellow tribesmen in the city, often in small social networks and voluntary associations, the individual with negative attitudes toward the government is encouraged in his views, and it is relatively easy to find participation channels that are consistent with them. In contrast, the case of the Kikuyu suggests that without participation opportunities and social support the estranged are not likely to be more or less active than anyone else.

Postindependence participation is more likely to be related to feelings of powerlessness and estrangement than is independence participation. A serious problem with the analysis here is that it tries to relate political attitudes and feelings at the end of 1967 to behaviors that may have taken place more than five years earlier, in considerations of the relationship between alienation and the independence participation style. None of the correlations involving these variables is very large and only one is significant. A great deal has taken place in the years since the independence movement was at its strongest. A number of intervening factors could operate to lower the relationships to the insignificant level where they now stand. Estrangement is measured as an orientation to the African government that rules Kenya in 1967, while participation in the independence movement may have reflected feelings about the colonial administration. Although we suggested how estrangement today may be related to participation in the independence movement, it is obvious that it also develops for a number of other reasons, such as ethnic group membership. To test these hypotheses properly, we would want to know how estranged an individual was from the colonial administration and how this attitude was related to participation in the independence movement.

Conclusions

Another way to evaluate the relationships between political participation and attitudes is to consider the meaning of participation in Kenya at a time when the processes of interest articulation and aggregation as well as demand satisfaction are just beginning to be institutionalized at the national level. Participation in national politics is either taking the place of or developing alongside of involvement in local authority structures, and one of the most significant aspects of this change is the growth of indirect, mediated, and representative forms of political communication, a situation that leaves many people feeling uneasy.

Members of parliament and city councillors in Nairobi frequently complain about the large number of people who come to see them seeking favors or assistance, the fact that many demands are impossible to satisfy, and that even if all demands were reasonable there are far too many for one man to handle, no matter how powerful. On the other hand, the constituents complain that the politicians do not really listen to the problems of the people and that, when they do, nothing is done about them anyway. One explanation for the difference in perspectives is that there is a great deal of articulation of demands in Nairobi but relatively little aggregation of them. That is, a large number of individuals approach politicians with requests, suggestions, or demands, which are almost always phrased in *individual* terms rather than in terms of the interests of some larger group. Therefore, if the politician manages to satisfy this demand, he has taken care of only *one* of his constituents. He cannot claim to have aided the member of a certain group, and thereby in the process helped *all* the members of the group. In addition, the fact that certain demands are not aggregated before they are brought to the politician means that there is a great deal of duplication in the requests that are made. The official feels a great deal of pressure after hearing the same complaints or demands from a large number of people. In many cases, if he were a better politician, he would attempt to translate the favors he does do for people into favors performed for one group or another, so that he could assert that he helped as many people as possible. Given the current resources of city councillors in Nairobi, and the current level of demands from their constituencies, politicians will have to begin translating the demands from their constituents and the satisfaction of these demands into the articulation and demand satisfaction of social groups larger than the individual or household if they want to get reelected at a higher rate than they have been since independence.

Participation in politics can produce high feelings of powerlessness and estrangement in this context where involvement and activity are not necessarily associated with instrumental results. Rather, the results are often either so ambiguous or so random that their interpretation within social groups in the city is of greater importance than what actually happens.

Politics, in this setting, is highly symbolized and takes place as much on the expressive as on the instrumental level.[16] Participation and interest are important, not just because of the possible effects on individuals' daily lives but also because of the intrinsic value of participation itself for some individuals. People develop attitudes and beliefs about politics and politicians only in part because of their own personal experiences with government. It appears that the ways in which their face-to-face social groups interpret political life is at least of equal importance.

This explanation may help account for the fact that at present political participation and political alienation in Nairobi are more highly related to social status, life-style, and ethnicity than they are to one another. Involvement therefore does not necessarily mean approval of existing political institutions. Luos are just as likely to be involved in politics as Kikuyus, but within each group attitudes to government and the way in which these attitudes are linked to activity are very different. Clearly, participation opportunities and social support, which are represented by these ethnic groups,[17] are highly divergent. Along with the identification of two distinct styles of political participation, this should reaffirm the multiplicity of reasons for, and forms of, political participation open to individuals.

Chapter 9 Politics and Social Life in Nairobi

Three commonly asserted dichotomies have been considered and found inadequate conceptualizations in this study of political attitudes and behaviors in Nairobi: (1) participation-alienation, (2) rural-urban, and (3) class-ethnicity. This chapter discusses our major findings through a critique of these three dichotomics. The opposition of participation-alienation is considered in terms of evidence about the behavioral basis of postindependence politics in Nairobi and the attitudinal orientations underlying it; the rural-urban opposition is discussed in light of our findings about the ways Nairobi residents participate in a wider social and political system than urban residence often implies; and the class-ethnicity opposition is evaluated in terms of our observation that these two priniciples of social organization operate together, rather than in contradictions to produce social and political networks in the city.

Participation-Alienation
As used in this study, neither participation nor alienation is a unidimensional concept, and theoretical conclusions must take this into account. The relationships between political behaviors and attitudes and the social context of Nairobi show the importance of not confounding the dimensions of each concept. For example, there is a striking difference between individuals who were likely to be active in the political independence movement and those who are the most active participants in the postindependence period. The former were likely to be the members of the urban mass, the relatively long-term urban residents, older, poorly educated with relatively low incomes, while the latter are more recent urban migrants, who hold good jobs, have relatively high salaries, and are well educated. In short, they are part of the newly educated urban elite, who are relatively familiar with bureaucratic structures and have the specific skills and training needed to operate within them.

Political participation in Nairobi has moved from the mass base that characterized politics in the independence struggle to a narrower, more elitist foundation in the postindependence period. The mass participation structures of electoral and party politics have been left to wither away as technical elites and powerful individuals seek to secure their hold on political office. For the most part, mass participation is seen as disruptive to the development process and as an obstacle to resolution of the problems facing the country. Many leaders argue that most people do not really understand the problems facing the country. They suggest that only a government of enlightened leaders can ensure progress. If the people are too closely involved in the decision-making process, the argument continues, they will want to spend money on relatively tangible projects—schools, roads, clinics, and so on—whereas only the technical elite understands that such projects must be balanced against the need for long-term development programs.

Thus, a new ideology is appearing which is used to support such actions as refusal to give the opposition party a right to hold any political rallies in its three years of existence, the arbitrary canceling of elections, the use of preventive detention, and other steps to keep the new elite securely in power. It is an ideology of "benevolent elitism," which sounds many of the same tones as the paternalism of the old colonialists. It allows the elite to separate themselves from the mass of the population by providing a rationale to justify their superiority.

Similarly, distinguishing between the two dimensions of alienation, estrangement, and powerlessness shows that each is related to a different social base. Feelings of estrangement, like attitudes about the kinds of changes in the living conditions since independence, and attitudes toward the problems of tribalism and corruption are most clearly related to differences between the major tribal groups in the city. In contrast, differences in feelings of powerlessness are most clearly a function of relative deprivation in the social structure. Last, the data show that within each tribal group the social variables that are related to each dimension of alienation are different.

Individuals who are powerless are not likely to be politically active in the postindependence period, while some estranged individuals are. In the former case, people who see relatively little prospect of changing their social and political environment do not become involved in politics. On the other hand, people who hold the most negative views of the politicians and the government are most likely to participate in politics, when there are both social support and institutional opportunities for them to express their views.[1] This does not mean, however, that it is possible to oppose the government overtly. Rather, people who engage in political activities, such as following the news about politics on the radio or in the newspapers, talking about politics with friends and relatives, and visiting government offices, tend to hold the most negative orientations.

The findings suggest the extent to which political behaviors and attitudes are affected by very immediate events in a new and fragile political system. The pattern of political participation, for example, has sharply shifted between the independence and postindependence periods. Before independence, it was in the interests of the politicians to mobilize the urban masses for visible and widespread political activity. A few years later, the same leaders are not at all interested in encouraging mass political activity or providing effective mechanisms to ensure widespread political participation in the city. Similarly, the tribal tensions in Nairobi between the Kikuyus and other groups, most notably the Luo, are not the same as those that characterized the preindependence political conflicts.

Public opinion and behavior are volatile and subject to widespread change in certain situations. Especially in recently independent countries, where political institutions and loyalties are weak, there are likely to be rapid changes in political attitudes and action as functions of specific local events. It also means that political traditions are relatively unimportant and that political leaders must constantly "deliver" in order to receive continued public support. Those who speak of past achievements will have as much trouble gaining public backing as those who promise that the rewards will come in the future.

Social Change and Rural-Urban Ties
Politics in Nairobi is taking place in a setting of rapid and uneven social change. The city has tripled in size in the last twenty years. It is the center of attention for most of the country; when important decisions are made, they are made in Nairobi. When a businessman wants a loan, he comes to Nairobi to talk to important people there. When a boy finishes school and begins to look for work, he usually starts in the capital.

In a city where social change is swift, it is also brutal; and some

people are much better prepared than others to absorb its shock. Social
change is not a unidirectional concept. It does not only mean progress,
growth, and expansion. Rather, it means that things are different from
one day to the next. It means that people must struggle to stay even.
It means that they must continually be ready to react and adjust. It
means that they live in a social environment with low levels of stability
and certainty.

People in Nairobi react to this situation by maintaining strong ties
with their relatives both in the city and in rural communities. These
links provide security in two ways: (1) as a source of help for individuals when they have problems in the city, and (2) as a rural alternative
to which they can turn if life in the city becomes too difficult. At
the same time that strong family ties serve to cushion some of the
shocks of social change, they also mean that individuals make conservative social decisions living in an environment they neither understand
nor control very well.

Relatives living in the city provide one another with the only form
of social insurance that is financially possible in Kenya today. While
the extent of obligation and assistance to relatives varies widely, there
are few people who deny the moral obligation to assist needy relatives
and who turn down all requests for assistance. To some extent, differences in levels of assistance follow ethnic lines. It is commonly asserted,
for example, that the traditional circle of obligation is much wider
for Luos than for Kikuyus. In the former case, obligations to children
of a father's sister or brother are almost as strong as those to a brother
or sister. Similarly, a man considers the children of his brother as his
own. In contrast, among the Kikuyu, obligations are usually limited
to one's own parents, children, and possibly siblings.

The result is that individuals have a relatively large number of
people to whom they can turn for assistance in emergencies. Likewise,
there are many people who turn to them, making it difficult for people
to accumulate capital. In effect, there is often a sort of leveling process
that takes place within families. A man is educated by his father and
gets a good job in the city. He then assumes the burden of paying the
school fees and supporting his younger brothers. They will then come
to live with him for a while in the city, and if the older brother is sick
or loses his job, they might assume the responsibility of seeing that his

children are clothed and that their school fees get paid. Or a younger
cousin comes to the city to look for work after finishing school. A man
will give him a place to sleep, food, and possibly clean clothes for
several months while he is job hunting. If in the end he is unsuccessful, the man may buy the bus ticket so he can get back home.

In addition to providing family-oriented social networks in the city,
close family ties mean that an individual always has a rural alternative
to which he can turn if life in the city become impossible. A person
who owns several acres of land in the rural areas can grow food to live
on, although he will have trouble paying school fees. An individual
with a larger farm probably lives comfortably in a rural community,
even though life may not be as exciting as it is in the city. Rural ties
are also important for helping individuals living and working in
Nairobi. A man may send several of his children to live with rural
relatives, thus reducing his cost of living in the city where food, clothing, and rent are all more expensive than in the rural community.
Thus, in the same way that rural relatives may stay with him when
they come to town, he can send members of his family to stay with
them in the countryside.

Individuals often use their income from the city to strengthen their
position in a rural community. Not only does the man working in the
city support rural relatives, but he also makes direct investments in
the rural areas. Most important, a man who has a good job in the city
and a chance to save money will usually buy land in the rural areas,
purchase animals for his farm, or invest in cash crops, such as coffee or
tea. Although he may live on the farm only a short time every year, it
is widely known that he intends to live there when he stops working
in the city. Furthermore, it is commonly accepted that he is living in
Nairobi because he "has to," as this is the best way to support his
family and prepare for the future.

In the same way that the system of mutual assistance and the acceptance of widespread obligations to relatives in the city is an inhibition
to saving and investment, the decision to invest savings in buying land
and improving existing farms is also conservative for several reasons.
First of all, it is conservative in the sense that it stresses the ties that
an individual has with the past, with his family, his clan, and his tribe.
Second, it is conservative in that it probably does not yield the highest

return for his capital. Instead of investing in a farm, an individual might buy a house in the city (either where his family can live or where he can rent rooms to others), or he might begin a business in Nairobi. The present scale of rents in the city (which will probably continue to go up steeply) guarantees a man an excellent return on his money if he is a houseowner, while ownership of a successful business can also be extremely profitable.

For the most part, the only people making sizable investments in either houses or businesses in the city are the Kikuyu. A common stereotype is that they are more ruthless and money hungry than any other group, but what seems more likely is that a combination of circumstances has served to make business investments more attractive to them in the immediate postindependence period. First, land pressure in Central Province is so severe that a Kikuyu who wants to buy land near his birthplace is often unable to do so. One alternative is to try to get land on a settlement scheme in the Rift Valley, but this is not always easy, and the returns from some of the schemes are often low because of the stiff repayment schedule. Thus, a Kikuyu with money to invest is not always able to buy land. Second the political situation has made it easier for Kikuyus to get loans. Third, the political climate has made the Kikuyus feel that Nairobi is "their city," while the other groups feel more and more that they are visitors in a foreign territory. For non-Kikuyus an investment in the city, therefore, is not safe and it means that they increasingly perceive the necessity to have an alternative in the rural areas if they should lose their jobs in the city (or be forced to leave).

Thus, Nairobi and the countryside are not seen by most people as two points on the rural-urban continuum. Rather, they are two locations within the same social system, and a person can move back and forth between them without severing his ties with either. A man moves away from the rural community by taking a bus into the city. However, the move does not mean that his obligations, responsibilities, and dependence upon the people in the rural communities are diminished. He continues to acknowledge this even after living and working in Nairobi for twenty or twenty-five years, and his rural relatives also recognize it. In addition, the modern transportation system makes it possible for an individual to move back and forth between the rural

and urban settings for short visits several times a year, and in cycles
that last a few years depending upon such factors as job availability,
the age of his children, and his own mood.[2]

In the city the fact that a person is constantly in contact with people
from other tribes does not mean that he is less a member of his own
ethnic group. Regardless of how long he has lived in town, or the
extent of changes in his patterns of dress or eating habits, a person
is likely to have his closest friends from his own ethnic community and
to continue to acknowledge his obligations to rural relatives. Participating in ethnically homogeneous social networks, individuals share the
news from the rural areas, celebrate traditional holidays, and generally
insulate themselves from losing their ethnic identity in the city.

Of the adults living in Nairobi today, 95 percent are migrants from
the rural areas. Under the colonial regime, limited opportunities and
low wages prevented the development of a large population, committed to city life, who consider Nairobi, rather than a rural district,
their home. In the past few years, however, this has changed as both
the adult male/female ratio and the adult/child ratio have decreased
and moved toward that found in the rest of the country. One effect of
these changes is that there is now growing up in Nairobi a generation
of children who were born and raised in the city. It will be interesting
to see in what ways they come to differ from the migrants of their
own and their parents' generations. On the one hand, assimilation
theory would suggest that ethnicity will be less important to them, and
that they will be much more oriented to urban life and urban social
solutions, maintaining relatively weak ties with people living in the
rural areas. The contrary hypothesis is that they are being socialized
into relatively closed, ethnically homogeneous social networks, that
they make periodic trips between the city and the rural areas with
their parents and other relatives, and finally that they will learn the
values of insecurity associated with city life from their parents. In this
case, they, like their parents, will identify strongly with their ethnic
group and participate in relatively homogeneous social institutions,
even if certain cultural manifestations of ethnicity, such as language,
food, or dress, diminish in importance to them.

The data presented here, and in many of the studies cited in Chapter
4, suggest that ethnic identifications, which provide an important basis

for social and political organization, are quite persistent. Individuals in the city selectively participate in urban institutions and have their closest contact with only a few people. While each generation may find the specific institutions or customs of their parents inappropriate, their reaction is usually to create new institutions that better serve their particular needs. The generation of children born and raised in Nairobi in the postindependence period is learning the importance of ethnic identification from their parents, as well as from their individual experiences in the city where "the ethnic facts of life" are often taught in blunt terms. Therefore, it is probable that ethnicity will continue to provide an important basis for political and social identification and action for the immediate future in Kenya.

Social Class and Ethnicity
In addition to ethnicity, this study showed the importance of social class differences in explaining patterns of political participation and alienation in the postindependence period. Social class differences in political participation are important as the uneducated and the poor are less involved than their high-status counterparts in political activities requiring specific skills. Increasingly, participation requires knowing how to cope with a government bureaucracy or the formation of an interest group that can effectively present a problem to government officials, and these skills are found disproportionately among the educated and relatively rich in Nairobi.

The leaders of the nationalistic independence movement are now the protectors of a developing system of social stratification. Rather than eliminating social differences, governmental programs, such as the expansion of primary- and secondary-school education and the Kenyanization of the government bureaucracy and private industry, have the effect of stratifying the African population and expanding class differences. A man with a government job paying Shs. 2,000/– a month, whose wife may also work as a schoolteacher or nurse, will have much less trouble educating his children than the man earning Shs. 225/– a month as a messenger. Because of his resources, the man with higher income can afford to send his son to a former European school, where he will have a better chance of learning English well, passing his examinations with high scores, and getting a good job.

Similarly, there are striking differences in life-style between the political leaders, in parliament, in local councils, in the administration, and the mass of the population. Furthermore, there has been little hesitation about using their political positions in order to ensure their economic security in the future. Thus, trading licenses, government-supported loans, and other forms of assistance have permitted the politicians to grow rich at the same time as their political power has mounted. Sklar noted the same process in Nigeria and wrote:

In power, the nationalistic parties helped to create a new pattern of social stratification. They sanctioned the liberal use of public funds to promote indigenous private enterprise, while many of their leading members entered upon a comparatively grand manner of life in parliamentary office.[3]

The mass public has been increasingly cynical about politicians and their maneuverings. Aware of this loss of support from the population, the political leaders have grown even more acquisitive, trying to take what they can "while the getting is good" for fear they may be turned out of power suddenly. At the same time, the political leaders have shown less and less hesitation to use governmental powers to protect powerful individuals. Preventive detention, selective allocation of development projects, outright corruption, canceled elections, and bureaucratic trickery all have been used to aid certain people and thwart any opposition. For example, when the government decided it did not want to contest the parliamentary elections in 1968, they were simply put off for two years. When the local government elections were held in 1968, the papers of all the opposition party candidates were declared "invalid" on various trumped up technicalities, thereby turning the election into a "no contest."

Social class is one principle that provides selective access to effective political action. A second is tribalism or ethnicity, which this study showed to be extremely important in understanding differences in political beliefs and attitudes in the postindependence period. Increasingly, the Kikuyu domination of the positions of power both inside and outside the government has led to more and more negative responses to the government on the part of members of other groups. The talk of how the Kikuyu are using their power to secure their position further, described as "Kikuyuization," is based upon both real

and imagined differences in the allocation of government loans, trade
licenses, plots on settlement schemes, the construction of new schools
and hospitals, and jobs. There is a widespread charge that Kikuyus in
the government are promoted faster than others even though they
often have lower skills and experience. In addition, there is the feeling
that a disproportionate share of government resources is spent in
Central Province, which is almost totally Kikuyu. For example,
Rothchild shows that a higher percentage of school-age children (between the ages of 7 and 13) are enrolled in schools in Central Province
than in any other area of the country.[4] In 1964, 94 percent of the
school-age children in Central Province were in school, while the
national average was only 58 percent.

The importance of tribal membership for politics is one of the
bitterest disappointments of the postindependence period, in the same
sense that the preindependence unity that prevailed among the larger
tribes (particularly the Kikuyu and Luo) proved to be of short dura-
tion. Political interests are often defined in terms of tribal or communal interests and do not extend beyond them. To the extent that
individuals have any faith in politicians, it is limited to leaders from
their own tribe. The experience in Nairobi since independence also
shows that contact between members of different ethnic groups does
not necessarily diminish suspicions and rivalries between them. Rather,
there is often a relatively high level of contact, on a day-to-day basis,
in which members of different groups find themselves competing for
scarce resources (for example, jobs or housing) so that contact in-
tensifies differences. There is widespread acceptance of the view that
if a person wants something done for him, he must find a fellow tribesman to do it.

Social class and tribe are not necessarily incompatible with each
other as principles of social and political division. In fact, the two can
operate at the same time in producing political divisions in a society.
Gordon[5] uses the term "ethclass" to describe social groupings based on
both principles in the United States.[6] As is illustrated in the hypothetical Table 9.1, individuals tend not only to be associated with
other people of their own ethnic group but also with people from their
own social status. People who are well educated tend to have friends
who are also well educated, while poor people also associate with other

Table 9.1. Hypothetical System of Social Stratification Based upon Social Class and Tribe in an African City

	Tribe A	Tribe B	Tribe C
White-Collar and Professional Class	1A	1B	1C
Working Class	2A	2B	2C
Urban Squatters	3A	3B	3C

poor people. At the same time, they also tend to associate with people from their own tribe. Thus, the two principles of class and tribe work together to form the emerging system of social stratification in Nairobi. The importance of one does not necessarily imply the unimportance of the other.

Both the rows and columns in the table can be considered social borders across which association at different frequencies is possible. By comparing the frequencies in both directions, we can determine the relative importance of each principle of association. In addition to representing social barriers to association, the rows and columns can also express probabilities of different groups holding similar attitudes and beliefs. Thus, the following sort of questions about associations and beliefs in a city can be asked: Are the urban squatters of one tribe more likely to have attitudes toward the government and politicians similar to those of urban squatters from another tribe or to members of their own tribe in the white-collar or working class? Will professionals from one tribe have closer personal relations with professionals from another tribe than with working-class people who are from their own tribe?[7]

Class and ethnicity have a different importance in different areas of political life. To illustrate this, the data in Table 9.2 show that political participation and information are related to class and not ethnicity, that attitudes toward the government since independence are a function of ethnicity, that assessments of living conditions since independence are determined by both class and ethnicity, and that formal group membership and the belief that politicians are overpaid are related to neither class nor ethnicity.

Social class and tribe are the most important variables in explaining political behavior and attitudes in Nairobi but not the only ones. Sex

Table 9.2. Class and Ethnicity as Predictors of Selected Political Attitudes and Behaviors

	Class	Ethnicity
Political participation—independence style	.001	n.s.
Political participation—post independence style	.001	n.s.
Number of ministers in cabinet named correctly	.001	n.s.
Has the government done more than you expected since independence?	n.s.	.001
Political estrangement	n.s.	.001
Since independence, what has happened to living conditions in the city?	.001	.001
Since independence, what has happened to your living conditions?	.001	.001
Number of formal group memberships	n.s.	n.s.
Do you think that politicians are overpaid for the work they do?	n.s.	n.s.

The significance levels presented in the table are based on the F-ratios from an analysis of variance.

differences, for example, are extremely important in explaining different levels of political participation, as men are much more likely to be politically active than women. By adding one or more additional variables to the illustration used in Table 9.1, we can also consider the differential importance of a variable, such as sex, across tribe or class. Thus, one hypothesis might be that sex differences in political participation would be weaker among the white-collar and professional class than among working-class individuals or urban squatters.

Conclusions

The data presented in this study of political behavior in Nairobi articulate the relationship between social life and politics in an African city. By presenting our findings in the form that we have, we hope to provide a benchmark against which changes in Kenyan politics can be measured, as well as a basis for comparison with other political systems. Political scientists, along with other observers, heralded the widespread changes that would result from political independence in Africa. This study is one step toward assessing the accuracy of their predictions. In addition, we have tried to turn the telescope around for a view of politics from the perspective of the mass public in an African city, to show their reactions to politics rather than the promises aimed at them by the political elite.

Appendix A Some Additional Comments on Sex Differences in Political Participation

The data presented in Chapters 6 and 7 showed that men tend to be more active politically than women and that, furthermore, political activity is associated with different life-style and social-status variables within each sex. The material presented in this appendix explores some of these relationships more carefully.

Participation and Rural Contact

Men engaged in both participation patterns more frequently than women, and when the relationship between participation styles and contact with the rural areas is examined separately for each sex some interesting differences appear. Among men, as is shown in Table A.1, those who participate more in each participation pattern have significantly higher contact with the rural areas than those with low participation scores. However, the components of the index associated most highly with each participation style are different. Men who send money to relatives in the rural areas and men who send money most frequently have the highest scores on the independence-style index. This relationship holds even when the effects of income are partialed,

Table A.1. Political Participation Styles by Contact with the Rural Areas Items by Sex

	Men		Women	
	Independence Style	Post-independence Style	Independence Style	Post-independence Style
Contact with the rural areas index	.17* (329)	.13† (330)	−.15† (168)	.12 (168)
Send money home in past year?	.25* (329)	.08 (329)	−.17† (168)	.16† (167)
How often did you send money home?	.28* (327)	.05 (327)	−.10 (166)	.15† (166)
Did relatives visit in the past year?	.13† (329)	.11† (329)	.00 (167)	.21* (167)
How many visited in the past year?	.00 (324)	.12† (324)	−.09 (165)	.05 (165)
Receive food in the past year?	−.03 (329)	.09 (329)	−.10 (167)	.28* (167)
How often received food?	−.07 (325)	.00 (325)	−.04 (167)	.19† (167)

* Significant at the .01 level.
† Significant at the .05 level.
Sample sizes in parentheses.

despite the fact that sending money home is a function of income. The postindependence style is related to whether or not relatives visited in the past year and the number of relatives visiting in the city.

Among the women the pattern is quite different. The independence-participation style is negatively related to contact with the rural areas, and sending money home suggested that women who were active in the independence movement were those with the greatest urban orientation and those without strong rural ties. These are the people who Austin suggests will join the independence movement. On the other hand, for women contact with the rural areas is unrelated to postindependence participation, although this style of participation is positively related to several components of the index: sending money home, the frequency with which money is sent home, receiving food from home, how often food is received, and having relatives from home visit in the city.

Men and women also differ in the ways in which friendship patterns in the city are related to participation. As is shown in Table A.2,

Table A.2. Participation Styles by Urban Friendship Patterns by Sex

	Total Sample		Men		Women	
	Independence Style	Postindependence Style	Independence Style	Postindependence Style	Independence Style	Postindependence Style
(1)	.05 (474)	−.13* (474)	.04 (316)	−.04 (316)	.13 (158)	−.23* (158)
(2)	.00 (469)	−.16* (469)	.00 (313)	−.18* (313)	.00 (156)	−.16† (156)
(3)	−.01 (451)	−.10† (451)	−.06 (305)	−.05 (305)	−.03 (146)	−.18† (146)
(4)	.02 (475)	−.14* (474)	.02 (316)	−.08 (316)	.14 (159)	−.13 (159)
(5)	.02 (472)	−.19* (472)	.04 (314)	−.25* (314)	−.08 (158)	−.18† (158)
(6)	.01 (462)	−.10† (462)	.05 (311)	−.11† (311)	−.06 (151)	−.16† (151)
(7)	.06 (477)	.10† (477)	.03 (318)	.16* (318)	.17* (159)	.07 (159)

* Significant at the .01 level.
† Significant at the .05 level.
Sample sizes in parentheses.
(1) First friend from estate of residence.
(2) First friend from same district of birth.
(3) First friend from same tribe.
(4) Percent of friends from same estate.
(5) Percent of friends from same birthplace.
(6) Percent of friends from same tribe.
(7) Percent of friends made in Nairobi.

friendship patterns are more associated with postindependence participation than with the independence style. For women, having the closest friend outside the estate of residence is more important than for men, while for men the development of friendships with people from another birthplace and from the city rather than home is most important.

Political Information
Men had significantly more political knowledge on three of the four items, and therefore it is useful to examine the correlates of political information separately by sex. The variables that are correlated with political knowledge for men in the sample are very similar to those that are related to postindependence-style participation. Each of the following variables was correlated positively with at least two of the four political information questions: education (3), income (3), cinema attendance in the past year (3), closest friend from a birthplace other than the respondent's (2), low age (2), short length of residence in the city (2), and high contact with the rural areas (2). Among the women, the pattern is not as straightforward. Out of six possible significant intercorrelations between the four measures, five are significant for the men, while only two are significant for the women. Among the men, three of the four—identification of the MP, the minister for East African Affairs, and the number of ministers correctly identified—were significantly related to the postindependence participation style, while none was significantly related to the independence pattern. For women, however, only the number of ministers named was significantly related to postindependence participation, while identification of the member of parliament was positively related to the independence style. None of the other correlations was significant.

Correct identification of the member of parliament among women was related to many of the variables associated with independence-style participation: older age, greater length of residence in the city, a greater percentage of life in the city, and lack of land in the rural areas. On the other hand, the number of ministers a person could name was negatively related to independence-style participation and positively related to postindependence style, cinema attendance, education, income, and lower age. Among women, the dichotomy between the long-term city resident, without land in the rural areas and with low education and income, is juxtaposed to the woman who is younger, better educated, and who attends the cinema downtown. The first type participated more in the independence-participation pattern, while the latter is more active in the postindependence style of participation. The first was better at identifying the MP for her constituency, a man associated with the history of the independence movement, while the second had a better general knowledge of the other political actors in the national government today.

Formal Group Membership

Social-status differences, such as education and income were not significantly related to the number of organizations an individual belonged to; however, they were important in combination with sex differences in predicting *which* organizations a person joined. Table A.3 shows that men are more likely to be members of a labor union, a welfare, district, or tribal association, and a sports club, while women are more likely to be church members. Among men, education is negatively related to membership in a labor union or a political party, while it is positively related to membership in churches, sports clubs, and other associations. For women, education is negatively related to membership in a political party but not to membership in any other associational groups. Women who are members of formal organizations are more likely to have a greater percentage of their friends from outside

Table A.3. Sex and Education by Formal Group Membership

		Education Level	
	Sex‡	Men	Women
Formal Group Index	.25* (498)	−.10 (326)	−.12 (166)
Union Member	.34* (491)	−.23* (322)	−.02 (163)
Welfare, District, or Tribal Association	.15* (492)	−.07 (323)	−.01 (163)
Church Member	−.12* (489)	.19* (322)	−.01 (161)
Political Party Member	.03 (490)	−.29* (322)	−.35* (163)
Sports Club Member	.20* (491)	.12* (322)	.11 (163)
Other Group Member	.05 (462)	.15* (302)	.13 (154)

* Significant at the .01 level.
Sample size in parentheses.
‡ A positive sign means that the men engaged in the activity to a greater degree.

their own tribe and from the city and have spent more of their life in the city, while for men these variables are not significantly related to group membership. Men who are members of more groups have a higher level of contact with the rural areas and are likely to be larger landowners. Women who are members of formal organizations operate in a larger social network within the city, while men who are members of these groups have stronger ties with the rural areas. Specifically they are more likely to have relatives visit them in the city, to send money home to their families in the rural areas, and to send money home more often (Table A.4).

Table A.4. Formal Group Membership by Contract with the Rural Areas, Length of Urban Residence, and Friendship Patterns by Sex

	Formal Group Membership	
	Men	Women
Contact with the Rural Areas	.18* (330)	−.02 (168)
Did Relatives Visit in Past Year?	.13† (329)	−.01 (167)
Send Money Home in Past Year?	.23* (329)	.07 (167)
How Often Send Money?	.25* (327)	.06 (166)
Number of Acres of Land	.11† (327)	.06 (167)
Length of Residence	.18* (329)	.24* (167)
Percent of Life in City	.18* (329)	.22* (167)
Percent of Friends from Tribe	−.09 (311)	−.18† (151)
Percent of Friends from City	.09 (318)	.19† (159)

* Significant at the .01 level.
† Significant at the .05 level.
Sample sizes in parentheses.

Appendix B
Interview Schedule and Sampling Procedure

Estate _____

House No. _____

Room No. _____

Date _____

Hello. I am a student at University College, Nairobi. I am working on
a project which is trying to learn about some of the changes that take
place in people's lives when they come to live in the city. We would be
very glad if you could help us by answering a few questions, so that we
could better understand the kinds of problems that people face living in
Nairobi. I want to assure you that any answers you give us will remain
completely private and confidential.

How many persons are 18 years of age or over? (If more than one member
of household) Which one of these is the oldest? second oldest? third
oldest? (List all members of the household in the grid below by showing
their ages from oldest to youngest. Then select the respondent according
to the last digit of the questionnaire number and circle the number showing the final selection of the respondent.)

QUESTIONNAIRE NUMBER

	Members		Last digit of questionnaire number									
	Age	Sex	1	2	3	4	5	6	7	8	9	0
Oldest			1	1	1	1	1	1	1	1	1	1
2nd Oldest			2	2	1	1	2	1	1	2	1	2
3rd Oldest			1	2	3	2	1	2	3	1	3	3
4th Oldest			3	1	2	4	1	4	3	2	1	2
5th Oldest			4	2	3	1	5	5	3	1	4	2
6th Oldest			2	5	4	6	6	3	1	4	2	6
7th Oldest			6	7	5	4	2	1	7	3	2	5
8th Oldest			7	1	4	6	5	3	2	8	1	7
9th Oldest			4	8	5	9	7	1	2	3	6	9
10th Oldest			8	10	1	6	7	5	3	9	4	2
11th Oldest			10	3	9	7	6	4	2	8	11	1
12th Oldest			11	7	12	5	10	2	6	1	9	3

1. SEX: Male...1 Female...2 2. AGE: (Get estimate if "Don't Know")___

3. Where were you born? (Which district) _____

4. TRIBE: _____

5. For how many years have you lived in Nairobi? _____

6. Are you now married? Single...1 married monogomous...2 married
   polygamous...3 divorced...4 separated...5 widowed...6
6. a. (IF MARRIED) Where is your wife (husband) living? Nairobi...1
       Outside Nairobi...2
   b. (IF OUTSIDE NAIROBI) In which district _____
       (IF MORE THAN ONE WIFE) _____
   c. (IF MARRIED) What tribe is your wife (husband)? _____

7. How many children do you have? _____
   a. (IF RESPONDENT HAS CHILDREN) How old is each of them? Where is
       each living these days?

Child	Age	District of Residence	Child	Age	District of residence
1.			6.		
2.			7.		
3.			8.		
4.			9.		
5.			10.		

Now I would like to ask you several questions about your family at home.

8. In the past year what period of time have you spent with your family
   at home? None...1 One week or less...2 One week to one month...3
   1-3 months...4 3-6 months...5 Over 6 months...6
   a. (IF SOME TIME SPENT OUTSIDE NAIROBI) How often did you travel
       home this past year? Never...1 Once...2 Several times...3
       Once a month...4 Once a week or more often...5

9. Have relatives from home come into Nairobi and visited you in the
   past year? Yes...1 No...2
   a. (IF YES) about how many people came to visit you? 0...1 1-5...2
       6-10...3 11-20...4 Over 20...5

10. Many families send food to their relatives living in Nairobi. In
    the past year has your family at home sent you any food? Yes...1
    No...2
    a. (IF YES) About how often did they send you food? Once a week
       or more...1 About once a month...2 Several times during the
       year...3 Once...4 Never...5

11. In the past year have you sent any money to help relatives at
    home? Yes...1 No...2

11. a. (IF YES) How often did you send money? Once a month...1 A
         few times this year...2 Once this year...3 Never...4

12. Some people receive a great deal of help from their relatives.
     Others find that relatives make too many requests for help. Do you
     think that if a man is to get ahead in Nairobi he must sometimes
     tell his relatives to leave him alone or not? Must tell relatives
     to leave him alone...1 Don't know...2 Must not tell them this...3

13. Now I am going to read to you a list of some of the ways in which
     people participate in politics. After I read each way people
     participate, please tell me whether you do these things these days.

	yes	no
Follow the news about politics on the radio	___	___
Follow the news about politics in the newspapers	___	___
Talk about politics with friends	___	___
Talk about politics with family and relatives	___	___
Attend political rallies or meetings	___	___

Now I will read some more ways in which people can participate and I
would like you to tell me if you have ever done any of these things.

	yes	No
Vote	___	___
Join a political party	___	___
Pay dues to a political party	___	___
Write a letter to a newspaper	___	___
Write a letter to your MP	___	___
Write a letter to your City Councillor	___	___
Visit a session of Parliament	___	___
Attend a City Council Meeting	___	___
Work for a candidate to get him elected	___	___
Go and see a government official when you had a problem	___	___

14. Have you ever met the M.P. from this constituency personally?
     Yes...1 No...2
     a. What is his name? _____ Incorrect...1 Correct...2

15. Have you ever met your City Councillor personally? Yes...1 No...2
     a. What is his name? _____ Incorrect...1 Correct...2

16. Are you at present registered on the new Electoral Roll? Yes...1 No...2
     a. (IF YES) In what constituency are you registered? Nairobi...1
         Outside Nairobi...2

17. Now I would like to ask you about organizations which you are a member.
     a. Are you a member of a trade union? Yes...1 No...2
         (IF YES) Which one? _____
     b. Are you a member of a district, welfare or tribal association?
         Yes...1 No...2
         (IF YES) Which one(s)? _____
     c. Are you a member of a church congregation? Yes...1 No...2
     d. How often do you go to church or mosque? More than once a
         week...1 Once a week...2 About once a month...3 Several
         times a year....4 Less often...5 Never...6

(IF ATTENDS SOMETIMES) Which church? _____

Where? (which estate) _____

e. Are you a member of a Sports Club? Yes...1 No...2

f. Are you a member of a political party? Yes...1 No...2

   (IF YES) Which one? KANU...1 KPU...2 Other____3 Refused answer...4

g. Are there any other organizations of which you are a member?

   Yes...1 No...2

   (IF YES) Which ones? _____

18. Think of your three best friends in Nairobi. In what part of the city (housing estate) are they living. From what district do they come? Are these people you met in the city or knew before you moved here?

Place of residence   District of origin   Friend from city or other place

1. _____

2. _____

3. _____

19. Should Kenya have an opposition party these days? Yes...1 Don't know...2 No...3

20. Since Independence do you think that the Nairobi City Council or the Central government has done more to improve people's lives in the city? Nairobi City Council...1 They have done the same...2 Central government...3 Don't know...4

21. Who is the person you would most like to see as Kenya's President after Mzee Jomo Kenyatta? _____ Your next choice? _____

22. Do you think there are things that person like yourself can do to get the government to change its policies? Yes...1 Don't know... No...3

23. Some people say that there are many MPs who do not listen to the problems of the people in their constituency. How satisfied are you that the MP from this constituency listens to the problems of the people here? (Read list)

               Are you satisfied...1
               Sometimes satisfied sometimes dissatisfied...2
               Dissatisfied...3
               (Don't know)...4

24. Recently President Kenyatta appointed a Minister for East African Affairs. Do you know his name? _____ Incorrect...1 Correct...2

25. Some people say that certain individuals or groups have so much influence over the way the government is run that the interests of the majority are ignored. Do you agree or disagree that there are such people or groups in Kenya today? Agree...1 Don't know...2 Disagree...3

(IF AGREE) What groups or people? _____

26. Do you think that the government really understands the problems of the people? Yes...1 Don't know...2 No...3

27. Some people say that politics and government are so complicated that the average man cannot really understand what is going on. In general, do you agree or disagree with that? Agree...1 Don't know...2 Disagree...3

28. In your opinion how serious is the problem of government officials and politicians doing special favors for their relatives and close friends (Read list):

    Very serious   ...1
    Serious   ...2
    Not important   ...3
    (Refused answer)...4
    (Don't know)   ...5

29. Since Independence do you think that living conditions in the city have (read list):

    Improved   ...1
    Remained the same...2
    (Don't know)   ...3
    Grown worse   ...4

30. Since Independence do you think that your living conditions (read list):

    Improved   ...1
    Remained the same...2
    (Don't know)   ...3
    Grown worse   ...4

31. To improve the lives of the people since Independence, has the government done: (READ)

    More than you had expected it would do...1
    About what you expected it would do   ...2
    Less than you expected it would do   ...3
    (Did not know what to expect)   ...4

32. Some people say that different groups have benefitted more than others from Uhuru. Which groups of people do you think have benefited the most? _____

    _____

    a. Which ones do you think have benefited the least? _____

    _____ __

33. Some people think that politicians are helping to eliminate the problem of tribalism in Kenya; others suggest that they are stirring

up tribal differences. Which do you think is most true? Trying
to eliminate tribalism...1 Don't know...2 They are doing both...3
Stirring up differences...4

34. How serious a problem do you think tribalism is in Nairobi today
(read list):
                    Very serious   ...1
                    Serious   ...2
                    (Don't know)   ...3
                    Not important ...4

35. Nowadays we hear a great deal about self-reliance. Do you think
there is a great deal that individuals can do to improve their lives
in the city? Yes...1 Don't know...2 No...3

36. How many Ministers in the Cabinet can you name? (stop at 8--record
in order named)
1._____   4._____   7._____
2._____   5._____   8._____
3._____   6._____

37. Do you think that politicians get too much money for the work that
they do? Yes...1 Don't know...2 No...3

38. Did you vote in the 1963 General Election? Yes...1 Don't remember...2
No...3
a. (IF YES) which party did you vote for? KANU...1 KADU...2
APP...3 Other...4

39. If there was an election today for which party would you vote?
KANU...1 Don't know...2 Refused answer...3 KPU...4 Other
(specify)_____5 Would not vote...6

40. In the past year have you ever attended any of the cinemas in the
city centre? Yes...1 Don't remember...2 No...3

41. Which is the highest standard or form in school which you successfully
completed? (write)_____ No school...1 Some primary...2
KPE...3 Form II...4 Form IV(School Certificate)...5 Higher School
Certificate or more...6

42. Do you have a shamba outside of Nairobi? Yes...1 No...2
a. (IF YES) In what district is it located? _____
b. (IF YES) How many acres is it? (Get respondent's estimate if
necessary) No shamba...1 1-3 acres...2 4-6 acres...3 7-10
acres...4 10-20 acres...5 Over 20 acres...6

43. What kind of work do you do? _____
a. (IF MARRIED) What kind of work does your wife(husband) do?_____

		Respondent	Wife/Husband
1.	Housewife	1	1
2.	Clerical/sales employee	2	2
3.	Small merchant/artisan/self employed	3	3
4.	Professional/business proprietor/ teacher/ higher government official	4	4
5.	Skilled worker	5	5
6.	Manual/unskilled/domestic worker	6	6
7.	Student	7	7
8.	Farmer	8	8
9.	Unemployed	9	9

    b. (IF UNEMPLOYED OR STUDENT) Where do you get money to live?_____

44. In which of the following groups would you say that the total monthly income of your family in Nairobi falls? (HAND CARD)

$$0-200/- \quad ...1$$
$$201/--300/- \quad ...2$$
$$301/--500/- \quad ...3$$
$$501/--800/- \quad ...4$$
$$801/--1,200/- \quad ...5$$
$$1,201/--2,000/- \quad ...6$$
$$\text{Over } 2,000/- \quad ...7$$

45. Do you think the respondent was:
Extremely cooperative...1 Helpful...2 Reserved...3 Suspicious and uncooperative...4

_____ Interviewer No. _____

46. Language of interview: English...1 Kiswahili...2 Vernacular...3

Sampling Procedure

The data presented in this study were gathered in 498 hour-long interviews conducted in Nairobi between December 8 and December 22, 1967, in the communities of Shauri Moyo and Kariokor. Twenty-two students (twenty males and two females) at University College Nairobi, enrolled in an introductory course in Social Research Methods, conducted the interviews.

The final interview schedule was developed after three different pretests in Nairobi. The first two were conducted during July and August 1966, and the second during November 1967. The sample sizes in the first three pretests were 120,100 and 44, respectively. The data from the second pretest were coded and punched at Northwestern University and analyzed during the 1966–1967 academic year, between the two field trips. The data from the other pretests were not analyzed in this fashion.

The interviewers used in the final version of the schedule were drawn from all of the major tribal groups in Kenya, as well as from Tanzania and Uganda. The interviewers were distributed throughout the two communities so that an equal proportion of interviewers from each tribal group worked in each of the communities.

In Shauri Moyo 288 living units were selected for the sample, and interviews were completed in 274 of these. There are 990 rooms in Shauri Moyo, in 170 different houses. Each room was assigned a number from 1 to 990, and then the first 288 different three-digit numbers, selected from a table of random numbers, indicated the rooms in which the interviews were to be conducted. There are 240 flats in Kariokor estate, and an attempt was made to interview in every one of them; 224 of the interviews were conducted. Respondents were randomly selected from persons over 18 years of age within each household according to the form found on the first page of the Interview Schedule.

The final version of the interview schedule was written in English. Then a Tanzanian student at the University translated it into Swahili. This Swahili version was brought to another Tanzanian who translated it into English. The two English versions were compared, and when there was a difference between the two versions, it was discussed with the two translators. In some cases the Swahili translation was altered, while in others, the English was modified so that a phrase or idiom could be translated into Swahili more accurately. Eight percent of the interviews were conducted in a vernacular language, when it was felt that the respondent was unable to understand properly either the English or Swahili. The proportion of interviews conducted in each estate in each language was quite different. In Shauri Moyo 13 percent were conducted in English, 74 percent in Swahili, and 13 percent in a vernacular language, while in Kariokor 86 percent were conducted in English, 12 percent in Swahili, and 2 percent in a vernacular. The percentages for the combined sample were 46 percent in English, 46 percent in Swahili, and 8 percent in a vernacular.

Notes

Chapter 1

1. An overview of the literature on political participation is found in Lester Milbrath, *Political Participation: How and Why People Get Involved in Politics* (Chicago: Rand McNally, 1965), passim; also relevant is Sidney Verba, Norman Nie, and Jae-On Kim, *The Modes of Democratic Participation: A Cross-National Comparison* (Beverly Hills, Calif.: Sage Professional Papers in Comparative Politics, 1971); and Sidney Verba and Norman H. Nie, *Participation in America: Political Democracy and Social Equality* (New York: Harper & Row, 1972).

2. For detailed references to the literature on political alienation, see the notes to Chapter 8. A good overview is found in Ada Finifter, "Dimensions of Political Alienation," *American Political Science Review*, 64 (June 1970), pp. 389–410.

3. The importance of these three dimensions as bases of social differentiation in urban settings is considered in Scott Greer, *The Emerging City* (New York: Free Press, 1962).

4. See for example, Milbrath, *Political Participation*.

5. Some writers on African cities have made a point of distinguishing between ethnicity (urban) and tribe (rural). This distinction is not adhered to here as we find more difficulty in separating the social than the spatial fields. Therefore, the two terms tend to be used interchangeably. For an elaboration of this argument, see Marc Howard Ross and Thomas Weisner, "Social Consequences of Rural-Urban Networks in Kenya," in John Harris and Myron Weiner (eds.), *Cityward Migration in Developing Countries* (forthcoming).

6. This is a study of Africans in Nairobi, and these generalizations would not hold up so well as if they are also applied to interracial situations between the African, Asian, and European communities.

7. The Kenya shilling was worth $.14 at the time of the research.

8. For a discussion of ways in which participant observation can provide systematic data as well as of how it can be used with other data collection procedures, see Jennie-Keith Ross and Marc Howard Ross, "Participant Observation in Political Research," *Political Methodology*, 1 (Winter 1974), pp. 63–88.

9. A systematic statement of the importance of multiple measurement is found in D. T. Campbell and D. W. Fiske, "Convergent and Discriminant Validation by the Multitrait-Multimethod Matrix," *Psychological Bulletin*, 56 (March 1959), pp. 81–105.

10. The research reported here was conducted during two stays in Nairobi, one from June–August 1966 and the second from July 1967 to March 1968. Statements concerning political events and politicians refer to the time of the research, not to today.

Chapter 2

1. An excellent overview of the literature on African cities is found in William John Hanna and Judith Lynne Hanna, *Urban Dynamics in Black Africa* (Chicago: Aldine Publishing Co., 1971).

2. For a detailed analysis of one such squatter community in Nairobi, see Marc Howard Ross, *The Political Integration of Urban Squatters* (Evanston, Ill.: Northwestern University Press, 1973); Marc Howard Ross, "Community Formation in an African Squatter Settlement," *Comparative Political Studies*, 6 (October 1973), pp. 296–328; and Marc Howard Ross, "Conflict Resolution Among Urban Squatters," *Urban Anthropology*, 3 (Spring 1974), pp. 110–136.

3. *Political Record Book.* Nairobi District, Commencing 1899. DC/NBI.1/1, p. 4. (Kenya National Archives.)

4. Mary Parker, *Political and Social Aspects of the Development of Municipal Government in Kenya With Special Reference to Nairobi.* (Nairobi: Colonial Office, n.d. [1949]), p. 259.

5. *Political Record Book,* Nairobi District, no number on page. A census conducted in 1906 gives the population as follows: Europeans (579), Eurasians (63), Goanese (510), Asiatics (3071), and Africans (9291).

6. See George Bennett. *Kenya: A Political History, the Colonial Experience* (London: Oxford University Press, 1963). Also see a history of Nairobi written on the occasion of the fiftieth anniversary of the city, James Smart, *Nairobi: A Jubilee History, 1900–1950* (Nairobi: *East African Standard,* 1950).

7. For a good description of the various housing estates, or neighborhoods, in Nairobi, and of land use in the city from the early years, see Kenneth McVicar, "Pumwani: Twilight of an East African Slum" (unpublished Ph.D. dissertation, University of California at Los Angeles, 1969). In addition he provides an excellent discussion of the present-day neighborhoods and their ethnic composition.

8. A term used to refer to urban Africans of coastal Kenyan origin. Their historical experience brought them into close contact with Arabic culture including Moslem religion and Arabic, a non-Bantu language, from which a large number of Swahili words have been borrowed.

9. *Annual Report of the District Commissioner, 1913–14.* No page number.

10. *Nairobi District Annual Report,* 1941, p. 6. The District Annual Report for 1943 states that there were 3587 school-age children in the city, a figure that is probably lower than the figure for 1941 because pressure during the war years forced Africans to send their families back to the rural areas.

11. See Waruhiu Itote, *Mau Mau General* (Nairobi: East African Publishing House, 1967) and the more scholarly version in Carl G. Rosberg, Jr., and John Nottingham, *The Myth of 'Mau-Mau': Nationalism in Kenya* (Nairobi: East African Publishing House, 1966).

12. *Annual Report of the African Affairs Department, 1953* (Nairobi: City Council of Nairobi, 1953), p. 86.

13. Ibid., p. 6.

14. For a review of Kenyan politics in the late colonial and early independence periods see Rosberg and Nottingham, *The Myth of 'Mau-Mau';* George Bennett and Carl Rosberg, Jr., *The Kenyatta Election: Kenya 1960–61* (London: Oxford University Press, 1961); and Cherry Gertzel, *The Politics of Independent Kenya 1963–8* (London: Heinemann, 1970).

15. Adapted from *Kenya Population Census, 1969,* Vol. I (Nairobi: Statistics Division, Ministry of Finance and Economic Planning, 1970), pp. 69–70.

16. In contrast to African groups where the proportion of the group living in Nairobi is always under 10 percent, the proportion of Kenya's Europeans, Asians, Tanzanians, and Ugandans in Nairobi is between one-fifth and one-half.

17. LeVine and Campbell suggest a number of propositions concerning the effect of intergroup contact in their study of ethnocentrism. Its effects often are mediated by intervening conditions, rather than directly shaping images and behaviors. Robert A. LeVine and Donald Campbell, *Ethnocentrism* (New York: John Wiley, 1972), passim.

18. *Nairobi District Annual Report, 1943,* p. 4. Also see Marrion W. Forrester, *Kenya Today: Social Prerequisites for Economic Development* (The Hague: Mouton and Co., 1962).

19. N. S. Mwenja, *City Council of Nairobi Planning Report. No. 1: Population* (Nairobi: Nairobi City Council, 1967), p. 9. An adult is defined as being 16 years of

age or older. Mwenja's data are based on the 1962 census. The 1969 census does
not indicate that the male/female ratio for adults is significantly lower than 1962;
however, the breakdowns reported in the published volumes do not present the data
by age, sex, and race.

20. *Kenya Population Census, 1962* (Nairobi: Government Printer, 1964–1966),
Vol. III, Table VIII.3.

21. There seems to be a bit of difference between the three data sources on this
variable. The *City Planning Report* says, "These figures indicate that 83.6 percent of
the African population within the former city boundary was born outside the city
limits." (P. 20.) The Kenya population census (Vol. III) reports that 9.1 percent
of the persons enumerated in Nairobi were born in the city. (Table VI.1, p. 39.)
A 10 percent sample of the 1962 census analyzed by the author places the
percentage of persons born in Nairobi at 12.8, but if the peri-urban areas (recently
incorporated into the city) are added, then the author's figures coincide with
that of the Kenya population census report but not with those in the city's report.

22. Adapted from *Kenya Population Census 1962*, Vol. III, Table IV.3, pp. 27–29.
The figures were taken from the graduated, rather than enumerated, population
distributions in that table.

23. *Kenya Population Census 1962*, Vol. III, Table VIII.3.

24. Ibid., Appendix IV (d).

25. In analyses conducted by the author on a 10 percent sample of the 1962
Nairobi census, there were small and unimportant differences between the major
tribal groups on all of these life-style characteristics, suggesting that the
structural impact of city residence was somewhat equal across African groups in
the population. For greater detail, see Marc Howard Ross, *Politics and Urbanization: Two Communities in Nairobi* (unpublished doctoral dissertation, Evanston,
Ill.: Northwestern University, 1968), pp. 51–54.

26. For an overview of the role of housing policy in Kenya from the colonial
period to the present, see Richard Stren, "The Evolution of Housing Policy in
Kenya," in John Hutton (ed.), *Urban Challenge in East Africa* (Nairobi: East
African Publishing House, 1972), pp. 57–96.

27. "On the Housing of Africans in Nairobi with Suggestions for Improvements,"
a report by Senior Medical Officer of Health and Municipal Native Affairs
Committee of the Municipal Council of Nairobi on 30 April 1941, p. 5.

28. Rosberg and Nottingham, *The Myth of 'Mau Mau,'* p. 205.

29. The Kikuyu, Kamba, Baluhya, and Luo constitute 31, 12, 25, and 25 percent of
Shauri Moyo, respectively, and 42, 6, 26, and 20 percent in Kariokor. The Kamba
are underrepresented in both areas, but particularly in Kariokor, and the Kikuyu
are a larger proportion there than in Shauri Moyo.

30. This list was compiled from personal observation, the records of the Shauri
Moyo Social Hall, and a list of African Independent churches operating in
Nairobi was compiled by David Barrett of the Research Division of the Christian
Council of Kenya. Not all of these churches met at the same time or in the same
place each week.

31. Many residents of Kariokor owned automobiles, while very few in Shauri
Moyo did. On Monday night, 24 February 1968, the author conducted a short
survey in each estate between 1:30 and 2 A.M., when it was assumed that almost all
of the residents would be at home. These were 98 automobiles parked in Kariokor,
while there were only 20 in Shauri Moyo, and 15 of them were outside the bars
and shops (which were closed by that time). There are 240 flats in Kariokor and
about 970 single rooms in Shauri Moyo.

32. These data are presented in Ross, *Politics and Urbanization*, p. 97.

33. Ross, ibid., p. 98.

34. J. Clyde Mitchell suggests that in assessing the importance of urban experiences in a person's life it is more fruitful to consider the percentage of his life that he has spent in the city since the age of 15, the age at which he conceivably might enter the labor force, rather than the percentage of his life that he has spent in the city. This, however, ignores the experiences of socialization into the urban environment an individual encounters during childhood. On an empirical level in this sample, however, there is little difference, as the two measures are highly correlated with each other (.88). There is also a strong correlation (.65) between age and length of residence in Nairobi. At first it would appear that such a correlation would be trivial, but it indicates that the younger adults were not raised in the city but tended to migrate there in their late teens or early twenties, the same pattern followed by the older residents. As the pattern of migration changes, and a greater number of children are born and raised in the city, the correlation between age and length of residence should grow lower. See J. Clyde Mitchell, "Urbanization, Detribalization and Stabilization in Southern Africa: A Problem of Definition and Measurement," in Daryll Forde (ed.), *Industrialization and Urbanization in Africa South of the Sahara* (Paris: UNESCO, 1956).
35. Ross, *Politics and Urbanization*, p. 99.

Chapter 3

1. The concept of life-style is adapted from Greer, who in turn, bases his discussion on earlier work by Wirth and Shevky and Bell. For the most part these authors have used life-style, social rank, and ethnicity as characteristics of urban areas and have been less interested in individual variation. Our interest, in contrast, is in using these three concepts to describe patterns of individual level differences. A second point is to recognize that while the concept of life-style may be general and comparative, its specific indicators are likely to vary across setting. For example, Wirth and Shevky and Bell suggest that urbanites are not homeowners. In Nairobi and most other African cities the opposite is the case. Individuals who purchase or build houses in the city are demonstrating a commitment to urban life, in contrast to those who use their savings to purchase land in the rural areas. See Louis Wirth, "Urbanism as a Way of Life," *American Journal of Sociology*, 44 (1938), pp. 1–24; Eshref Shevky and Wendell Bell, *Social Area Analysis* (Stanford, Calif.: Stanford University Press, 1955); and Scott Greer, *The Emerging City* (New York: Free Press, 1962).
2. A good discussion of the development of measures of life-style for neighborhood urban units in social area analysis is by Wendell Bell, "Urban Neighborhoods and Individual Behavior," in Paul Meadows and Ephraim H. Mizruchi (eds.), *Urbanism, Urbanization and Change: A Comparative Perspective* (Reading, Mass.: Addison-Wesley, 1969), pp. 120–146.
3. The amount of land an individual owns in the rural areas is also positively related to education and income, $r = .15$ and .22, respectively.
4. The pattern is much more similar to the urbanization experience of American blacks where there is often frequent movement between the northern cities and southern rural communities, especially among the generation that first migrated north.
5. See, for example, Lorene Fox (ed.), *East African Childhood* (Nairobi: Oxford University Press, 1967).
6. Wages for an *ayah* in the African areas of the city range from Shs. 25/- to 75/- per month, a sum that is far below the minimum wage in the city of 175/- per month.
7. A good discussion of this question in general in African cities is found in A. W.

Southall. "Introductory Essay," in A. W. Southall (ed.), *Social Change in Modern Africa* (London: Oxford University Press, 1960), pp. 46–66.

8. R. Mugo Gatheru. *Child of Two Worlds: A Kikuyu's Story* (Garden City, N.Y.: Anchor Books, 1965), pp. 99–100.

9. Personal interview with informant.

10. Each respondent was asked the questions shown in Table 3.1, which provided the basis for an index measuring the intensity of contact with the rural areas. Questions 1, 4, 6, and 8 were used in the index because of the problem of redundancy. Each pair of items is tapping the same behavior so that in the last three pairs the second item was selected because of the greater detail in the response categories. In the first pair item 1 was selected because it was felt that the number of times a person visited home was more a function of distance than was the amount of time spent at home. The four items were factor analyzed, only a single factor was extracted, thereby indicating unidimensionality. The four items were weighted equally and scored in the same direction, and an index for each respondent was constructed. For a description of factor analysis in constructing indices, see Donald G. Morrison, Donald T. Campbell, and Leroy Wolins, "A Fortran IV Program for Evaluating Internal Consistency and Single-Factoredness in Sets of Multi-Level Attitude Items" (Evanston, Ill.: Northwestern University, Vogelback Computing Center, n.d.).

11. The correlation coefficents presented in this and succeeding tables are Pearson product moment correlations. Although many of the variables used here are ordinal rather than interval, the Pearson r is used because of easier interpretability, comparability, presentation, and evidence that violation of the assumption of normally distributed interval data does not produce serious problems unless we are also interested in estimating population parameters for these variables, which is not our case. If anything, our procedure is a conservative one in that our correlations will be artificially low, and the maximum absolute value of r less than ±1.00 depending upon the marginal distributions of the variables. Quinn McNemar, *Psychological Statistics*, 3rd ed. (New York: John Wiley, 1962), pp. 188–202; and William L. Hays, *Statistics for Psychologists* (New York: Holt, Rinehart and Winston, 1963), pp. 510–511, 536–538.

12. Remi Clignet and Joyce Sween, "Social Change and Type of Marriage," *American Journal of Sociology*, 75 (1969), pp. 123–145.

13. For an excellent discussion of the concept of social network and its application to urban Africa, see J. Clyde Mitchell (ed.), *Social Networks in Urban Situations* (Manchester: Manchester University Press, 1969).

14. Each respondent was asked the following question: "Think of your three best friends in Nairobi. In what part of the city (housing estate) are they living? From what district do they come? Are these people you met in the city or knew before you moved here?"

15. $r = 18$ ($N = 475$).

16. The districts of the major tribes in Kenya are tribally homogeneous, and therefore the tribe of the respondent's friends was inferred on the basis of their birthplace. In cases where the respondent reported that his closest friends were born in Nairobi, the case was dropped. This represented only 3 percent of the total number of friends mentioned (41 out of 1345). Additional data on the relationship between ethnicity, social status, and friendship choices are presented in the following chapter.

17. This finding contrasts with those which indicate that the dimensions of social status and life-style are independent in western American cities. Clignet and Sween, comparing census data from San Francisco, Rome, Accra, and Abidjan suggest that, as the scale of a society increases, increasing social differ-

entiation occurs, and the different bases of differentiation grow increasingly
independent of one another. They found that the discriminative power and
independence of social rank and life-style are greater in two western cities, San
Francisco and Rome, than in the two African ones, and related these differences to
variations in the scale of the societies in which each is located. Their finding
is based on aggregate data using census traits as the unit of analysis in contrast
to the finding here based on individual level correlations. Remi Clignet and Joyce
Sween, "Accra and Abidjan: A Comparative Examination of the Theory of the
Increase in Scale," *Urban Affairs Quarterly*, IV (March 1969), pp. 297–324.

Chapter 4

1. Michael Parenti makes a similar distinction between ethnicity as a cultural
phenomenon and a social one. He analyzes the concept with reference to American
cities, applying the three levels of analysis—the cultural, the social, and the
psychological—in the Parsonian system. Michael Parenti, "Ethnic Politics and the
Persistence of Ethnic Identification," *American Political Science Review*, 61
(September 1967), pp. 717–726.
2. One of the interesting aspects of this bloc voting is that it is not just a case of
people supporting a candidate of their own ethnic group. Instead, ethnic groups
tend to react as a unified social group to certain candidates. Thus, John F.
Kennedy received a higher proportion of the Jewish than Irish Catholic votes in
1960. Also, see Raymond E. Wolfinger, "The Development and Persistence of Ethnic
Voting," *American Political Science Review*, 59 (December 1965), pp. 896–908.
3. J. Clyde Mitchell, *The Kalela Dance: Aspects of Social Relationships among
Urban Africans in Northern Rhodesia*, Rhodes-Livingstone Papers, No. 27
(Manchester: Manchester University Press, 1956), p. 30.
4. Immanuel Wallerstein, "Ethnicity and National Integration in West Africa,"
in Pierre L. van den Berghe (ed.), *Africa: Social Problems of Change and Conflict*
(San Francisco: Chandler Publishing Co., 1965), p. 473. For this reason Wallerstein
suggests that we use the term "tribe" for the group in the rural areas, and ethnic
group for the one in the towns. Pp. 474–475.
5. Mitchell, *The Kalela Dance*.
6. See, for example, Kenneth Little, *West African Urbanization: The Study of
Voluntary Associations in Social Change* (London: Cambridge University Press,
1965).
7. A survey of independent church activity in Nairobi was carried out in July 1967,
and at that time 46 different congregations were located. Cecilia Irvine, "Report
on a Survey of African Independent (Separatist) Congregations in Nairobi City—
July 1967." Unpublished manuscript.
8. The Kirinyaga Welfare Association in Nairobi, for example, has a group of
Kikuyu elders who listen to disputes between individuals living in the city. Cases,
however, must be brought before them by both parties before a case is considered.
For a discussion of the effect of urban life on decision-making patterns among
tribal elders, see Marc Howard Ross, "Conflict Resolution Among Urban Squatters,"
Urban Anthropology, 3 (Spring 1974), pp. 110–136.
9. Daniel Lerner, *The Passing of Traditional Society: Modernizing the Middle East*
(Glencoe, Ill.: Free Press, 1958).
10. The concept of opinion leaders was first explored in the 1940 election study in
Erie County. See Paul Lazarsfeld et al., *The People's Choice* (New York: Columbia
University Press, 1948). It was further refined in their 1948 Elmira study, Bernard
Berelson et al., *Voting* (Chicago: University of Chicago Press, 1954), and admirably
summarized in Elihu Katz and Paul Lazarsfeld, *Personal Influence* (New York:

Free Press, 1956); also see Elihu Katz, "The Two-Step Flow of Communication: An Up to Date Report on a Hypothesis," *Public Opinion Quarterly,* 21 (Spring 1955), pp. 61–78.

11. A good discussion of the effect of contact between ethnic groups on images and ethnic hostility is found in Robert A. LeVine and Donald Campbell, *Ethnocentrism* (New York: John Wiley & Sons, Inc. 1972); also see John Hardin et al., "Prejudice and Ethnic Relations," in Gardner Lindzey and Elliot Aronson (eds.), *The Handbook of Social Psychology,* 2nd ed., Vol. 5 (Reading, Mass.: Addison-Wesley, 1969), pp. 1–76.

12. See, for example, Oscar Handlin, *The Uprooted* (New York: Grosset and Dunlap, 1951).

13. See, for example, Philip Mayer, *Townsmen or Tribesmen: Conservatism and the Process of Urbanization in a South African City* (Cape Town: Oxford University Press, 1963); Max Gluckman, "Tribalism in Modern British Central Africa," in Immanuel Wallerstein (ed.), *Social Change: The Colonial Situation* (New York: John Wiley & Sons, Inc., 1966), pp. 249–250; Herbert J. Gans, *The Urban Villagers* (New York: Free Press, 1962); and Nathan Glazer and Daniel Patrick Moynihan, *Beyond the Melting Pot* (Cambridge, Mass.: MIT Press, 1963).

14. Louis Wirth, *The Ghetto* (Chicago: University of Chicago Press, 1956).

15. Herbert J. Gans, "Park Forest: The Birth of a Jewish Community," *Commentary,* 11 (April 1951), pp. 330–339.

16. Pierre L. van den Berghe, "Towards a Sociology of Africa," in van den Berghe (ed.), *Africa: Social Problems of Change and Conflict,* pp. 78–79. For additional discussion of the pluralist position, see Leo Kuper, "Plural Societies: Perspectives and Problems," in Leo Kuper and M. G. Smith (eds.), *Pluralism in Africa* (Berkeley and Los Angeles: University of California Press, 1969), pp. 7–26; M. G. Smith, "Social and Cultural Pluralism," in van den Berghe (ed.) *Africa,* pp. 58–76; M. G. Smith, "Institutional and Political Conditions of Pluralism," in Kuper and Smith, *Pluralism in Africa,* pp. 27–65; and Pierre van den Berghe, "Pluralism and the Polity: A Theoretical Explanation," in Kuper and Smith, ibid., pp. 67–81.

17. For more detail concerning both the subjective and objective aspects of ethnicity in Nairobi, see Marc Howard Ross, "Measuring Ethnicity in Nairobi," in William M. O'Barr, David H. Spain, and Mark A. Tessler (eds.), *Survey Research in Africa* (Evanston, Ill.: Northwestern University Press, 1973), pp. 160–167.

18. Gluckman, "Tribalism in Modern British Central Africa," in Wallerstein (ed.) *Social Change: The Colonial Situation,* p. 251.

19. Wallerstein, "Ethnicity and National Integration in West Africa," in van den Berghe (ed.), *Africa,* p. 477, citing A. L. Epstein, *Politics in an Urban African Community* (Manchester: Manchester University Press, 1958), p. 231.

20. Wallerstein, in van den Berghe, *Africa,* p. 477.

21. Van den Berghe, *Africa,* pp. 83–84.

22. John Osogo, *History of the Abaluhya* (Nairobi: Oxford University Press, 1967).

23. Aidan Southall, "Introductory Essay," in A. Southall (ed.), *Social Change in Modern Africa* (London: Oxford University Press, 1961), p. 39.

24. Mayer, *Townsmen or Tribesmen,* p. 4.

25. Mayer, ibid., p. 99.

26. Glazer and Moynihan, *Beyond the Melting Pot.*

27. A. L. Epstein, *Politics in an African Urban Community* (Manchester: Manchester University Press, 1958); Gluckman, *Custom and Conflict in Africa,* Mitchell, *The Kalela Dance.*

28. Another good study of how situational selection operates with respect to

ethnicity in Africa is by Robert Melson, "Ideology and Inconsistency: The 'Cross Pressured' Nigerian Worker," *American Political Science Review*, 65 (March 1971), pp. 161–171.

29. See Eugene Webb et al., *Unobtrusive Measures* (Chicago: Rand McNally, 1966).

30. See, for example, Richard Sklar, *Nigerian Political Parties* (Princeton, N.J.: Princeton University Press, 1963). Sklar develops the concept of the "political class," a term he borrows from Mosca. The political class is not necessarily coterminous with the economic elite, but in many cases the two coincide.

31. Milton Gordon, *Assimilation in American Life: The Role of Race, Religion and National Origins* (Fairlawn, N.J.: Oxford University Press, 1964).

32. Eshref Shevky and Wendell Bell, *Social Area Analysis* (Stanford, Calif.: Stanford University Press, 1955). They examined the changing composition of San Francisco from 1940 to 1950. Others have found similar results looking at other U.S. cities. See Scott Greer, *The Emerging City* (New York: Free Press, 1962).

33. Abner Cohen's study of Hausa migrants in Ibadan involved in what he terms "retribalization" is an excellent example of a situation where over several generations markers of ethnicity shift dramatically. Cohen shows that in response to the social and political conditions of Ibadan life, Hausa ethnicity was refined as a way of maintaining group solidarity and economic domination of the long-distance trade in the city. Abner Cohen, *Custom and Politics in Urban Africa* (Berkeley and Los Angeles: University of California Press, 1969).

34. Wallerstein, "Ethnicity and National Integration in West Africa," in van den Berghe (ed.), *Africa*. For a good discussion about how markers and borders are related, see Jennie-Keith Ross, "Social Borders: Definitions of Diversity," *Current Anthropology*, 16 (March 1975), pp. 53–72.

35. The thrust of our argument has been that ethnicity is socially defined, that because of situational selection its importance can vary sharply across social and political settings, and that its markers, and sometimes even its borders, are redefined over time. Therefore, it is important to go beyond so-called "objective" measures of ethnicity to develop a more subjective, perceptual definition as well. See Marc Howard Ross, "Measuring Ethnicity in Nairobi," in O'Barr, Spain, and Tessler (eds.), *Survey Research in Africa*. In addition, our argument leads us to note that indeed there will be social situations where ethnic borders are quite unclear (that is, borders not highly defined and markers not recognized), or where there may be large-scale movements back and forth across borders. In such situations the efforts of social scientists to identify ethnic groups clearly are more likely to be unsuccessful. Such results are not necessarily methodological problems but rather an indication of an important dimension on which ethnicity can vary across societies: the degree of border definition between ethnic groups. Jennie-Keith Ross, "Social Borders: Definitions of Diversity"; Fredric Barth (ed.), *Ethnic Groups and Boundaries* (Boston: Little, Brown and Company, 1969); Aidan Southall, "The Illusion of Tribe," in Peter C. W. Gutkind (ed.), *The Passing of Tribal Man in Africa* (Leiden, Netherlands: E. J. Brill, 1970); Michael Moerman, "Who are the Lue?," *American Anthropologist*, 67 (1964), pp. 1215–1230; and Raoul Naroll, "Who the Lue Are," in June Helm (ed.), *Essays on the Problem of Tribe: Proceedings of the American Ethnological Society* (Seattle, Wash.: University of Washington Press, 1967), pp. 72–82.

36. An elaboration of this point is found in Marc Howard Ross, "Class and Ethnic Bases of Political Mobilization in African Cities" in William John Hanna (ed.), *The Quality of Urban Life* (Miami: University of Miami Press, 1975).

37. There is no significant difference between class and ethnic groups in this pattern, and therefore the data are pooled across groups.

Chapter 5

1. Greater detail concerning recent Kenyan political history is found in George Bennett and Carl Rosberg, *The Kenyatta Election: Kenya 1960–1961* (London: Oxford University Press, 1961); Cherry Gertzel, *The Politics of Independent Kenya, 1963–8* (London: Heinemann, 1970); Colin Leys, "Politics in Kenya: The Development of Peasant Society," *British Journal of Political Science*, 1 (1971), pp. 307–337; Henry Bienan, *Kenya: The Politics of Participation and Control* (Princeton, N.J.: Princeton University Press, 1974); and Goran Hyden, Robert Jackson, and John Okumu (eds.), *Development Administration: The Kenyan Experience* (Nairobi: Oxford University Press, 1970).
2. Each respondent was asked the following two questions:
1. "Since independence do you think that living conditions in the city have: (1) improved, (2) remained the same, or (3) grown worse?" and
2. "Since independence do you think that your living conditions have: (1) improved, (2) remained the same, or (3) grown worse?"
3. There is a .56 correlation ($N = 498$) between the two items. A "Don't Know" response was coded as the intermediate position—remained the same—on both questions.
4. The first two questions used are those mentioned earlier in Note 2. The third question was: "To improve the lives of the people since independence, has the government done (1) more than you expected it would do, (2) about what you expected it would do, or (3) less than you expected it would do?"
5. The correlation between contact with the rural areas and income is .29 ($N = 484$) and between contact and education is .20 ($N = 492$).
6. See Donald Rothchild, "Ethnic Inequalities in Kenya," *The Journal of Modern African Studies*, 7 (1969), pp. 689–711.
7. A "Don't Know" response was coded as intermediate on all three questions.
8. The following five items make up the political estrangement scale:
1. "Some people say that there are many MPs who do not listen to the problems of people in their constituency. How satisfied are you that the MP from this constituency listens to the problems of the people here? (Read List) (1) Satisfied, (2) Sometimes satisfied and sometimes dissatisfied, or (3) Dissatisfied."
2. "Some people say that certain individuals or groups have so much influence over the way the government is run that the interests of the majority are ignored. Do you agree or disagree that there are such people or groups in Kenya today?" (1) Agree, (2) Don't know, (3) Disagree.
3. "Do you think that the government really understands the problems of the people?" (1) Yes, (2) Don't know, (3) No.
4. To improve the lives of the people since independence, has the government done: (Read list) (1) More than you had expected it would do, (2) About what you had expected it would do, or (3) Less than you expected it would do?"
5. "Do you think that politicians get too much money for the work that they do?" (1) Yes, (2) Don't know, (3) No.
When the five items were factor analyzed, only a single factor was extracted, indicating unidimensionality.
9. Each respondent was asked if he is a member of a trade union, welfare, district, or tribal association, church congregation, sports club, political party, or other association. Each respondent is then given a score based on his total number of memberships.
10. David Parkin, *Neighbors and Nationals in an African City Ward* (Berkeley and Los Angeles: University of California Press, 1969); and David J. Parkin, "Tribe as Fact and Fiction in an East African City," in P. H. Gulliver (ed.), *Tradition*

and Transition in East Africa (London: Routledge & Kegan Paul, 1969).
11. Daniel Lerner, *The Passing of Traditional Society* (Glencoe, Ill.: Free Press, 1958).
12. The following two items make up the scale of political powerlessness:
1. "Do you think there are things that a person like yourself can do to get the government to change its policies?" (1) Yes, (2) Don't know, (3) No.
2. "Nowadays we hear a great deal about self-reliance. Do you think there is a great deal that individuals can do to improve their lives in the city?" (1) Yes, (2) Don't know, (3) No.
13. A number of other studies have suggested that political alienation is a multidimensional concept. See Joel Aberbach, "Alienation and Political Behavior," *American Political Science Review*, 63 (March 1969), pp. 86–99; Ada Finifter, "Dimensions of Political Alienation," *Amerian Political Science Review*, 64 (June 1970), pp. 389–410; Arthur G. Neal and Soloman Rettig, "On the Multidimensionality of Alienation, "*American Sociological Review*, 32 (February 1967), pp. 54–64; and J. L. Simmons, "Some Intercorrelations Among 'Alienation' Measures," *Social Forces*, 44 (March 1966), pp. 370–372.

Chapter 6

1. For good discussions of the concept of societal scale, see Godfrey and Monica Wilson, *The Analysis of Social Change: Based on Observations in Central Africa* (New York: Cambridge University Press, 1965); Scott Greer, *The Emerging City* (New York: Free Press, 1962), Chapter 2; and Leo van Hoey, "The Coercive Process of Urbanization: The Case of Niger," in Scott Greer et al. (eds.), *The New Urbanization* (New York: St. Martin's Press, 1968).
2. Wilson and Wilson, *The Analysis of Social Change,* p. 30.
3. The political machine is an excellent example of a local organization that recruits participants disproportionately from those residents of a community who have low scale positions.
4. For a review of the major findings concerning participation, see Lester Milbrath, *Political Participation* (Chicago: Rand McNally and Co., 1965).
5. This use of factor analysis in scale construction is discussed in Donald G. Morrison, Donald T. Campbell, and Leroy Wolins, "A Fortran IV Program for Evaluating Internal Consistency and Single-Factoredness in Sets of Multi-Level Attitude Items" (Evanston, Ill.: Northwestern University, Vogelback Computing Center, n.d.).
6. The following two items were dropped in the final construction of the scales as neither loaded highly on either factor: "Have you ever met the MP from this constituency personally?" and "Have you ever met your city councillor personally?"
7. These results hold when ethnicity is coded as a dummy variable and correlated with participation and when an F-test is run to compare mean participation scores of each group. Considering ethnicity as a subjective variable, as suggested in Chapter 4, also yields the same results, as both forms of participation are unrelated to whether or not an individual named a member of his own tribe for the next president or as the first cabinet minister he named. Having one's closest friends from one's own ethnic group is unrelated to independence participation and only slightly correlated to the postindependence style (−.10, N = 451 for first friend, and −.10, N = 462 for percentage of three friends, both significant at the .05 level).
8. William Kornhauser, *The Politics of Mass Society* (Glencoe, Ill.: Free Press, 1959), p. 212.
9. Dennis Austin, *Politics in Ghana, 1946–1960* (New York: Oxford University Press, 1964), p. 17.

10. Both styles of participation are significantly correlated with age, although the direction of the correlation differs in the two cases. Age is much more strongly associated with the independence style (.40) than with the postindependence style (–.09). Age is also negatively associated with education (–.41) and income (–.21), so that partialing for the effects of age on the relationship between participation and social status produces the following first-order partials:

	Participation Style	
	Independence	Postindependence
Income	–.06	.18*
Education	–.20*	.30*

*Significant at the .01 level.

Education continues to be associated with both forms of participation, while income is now related only to postindependence participation. The relationship between age and participation would probably be even stronger today, as these data were collected only four years after independence.

11. Austin, *Politics in Ghana.*

12. Richard Sklar and C. S. Whitaker, Jr., "Nigeria," in James S. Coleman and Carl G. Rosberg, Jr. (eds.), *Political Parties and National Integration in Tropical Africa* (Berkeley and Los Angeles: University of California Press, 1966), p. 620.

13. Remi Clignet and Joyce Sween, "Accra and Abidjan: A Comparative Examination of the Theory of Increase in Scale," *Urban Affairs Quarterly,* 4 (March 1969), pp. 297–324; and Dennis McElrath, "Societal Scale and Social Differentiation," in Scott Greer et al. (eds.), *The New Urbanization* (New York: St. Martin's Press, 1968).

Chapter 7

1. For a summary of findings in American politics, see Robert Lane and David Sears, *Public Opinion* (Englewood Cliffs, N.J.: Prentice-Hall, 1965), Chapters 2–4; and Lester Milbrath, *Political Participation* (Chicago: Rand McNally and Co, 1965).

2. Each respondent was asked, "Have you ever met the MP from this constituency personally? What is his name?," "Have you ever met your city councillor personally? What is his name?," "Recently President Kenyatta appointed a minister for East African Affairs. Do you know his name?," and "How many ministers in the cabinet can you name?"

3. Kenneth Little, "The Role of Voluntary Associations in West African Urbanization," *American Anthropologist,* 59 (1957), p. 593.

4. Ibid., pp. 588–589.

5. Ibid., pp. 591–592.

6. Each respondent was asked, "Now I would like to ask you about organizations of which you are a member. Are you a member of a trade union? Are you a member of a district, welfare or tribal association? Are you a member of a church congregation? Are you a member of a sports club? Are you a member of a political party? Are there any other organizations of which you are a member?" The formal organization index is the total number of organizations of which an individual reported being a member.

7. There are no significant differences between ethnic groups in their tendency to join voluntary associations, although we do find ethnic differences in the *types* of memberships people hold. Luos are far more likely to participate in

clan, tribal, and welfare associations, while Kikuyus report higher rates of membership in trade unions and political parties. There are also small but not significant differences in the propensity to be church members, joining sports clubs, and other associations, with Luos more likely to join these types of organizations than Kikuyus.

8. Appendix A presents the tables on which the discussion in this section is based, showing ways in which males and females in Nairobi have different social correlates of political participation and interest.

9. This does not rule out the possibility that different mechanisms may explain the relationship within each group, however.

10. The only significant relationship between independence participation and friendship choices for either sex is that women who show the highest levels of participation have the greatest proportion of their friends from the city, a function of their longer length of residence.

11. This point is explored more completely in Marc Howard Ross and Thomas S. Weisner, "Some Social Consequences of Rural-Urban Ties in Kenya," in John Harris and Myron Weiner (eds.), *Cityward Migration in Developing Countries* (forthcoming).

Chapter 8

1. For a discussion of the concept of alienation in general and political alienation in particular, see Joel D. Aberbach, "Alienation and Political Behavior," *American Political Science Review*, 63 (March 1969), pp. 86–99; Dwight G. Dean, "Alienation and Political Apathy," *Social Forces*, 38 (March 1960), pp. 185–189; Dwight G. Dean, "Alienation: Its Meaning and Measurement," *American Sociological Review*, 26 (October 1961), pp. 753–758; William Erbe, "Social Involvement and Political Activity: A Replication and Elaboration," *American Sociological Review*, 29 (April 1964), pp. 198–215; Ada W. Finifter, "Dimensions of Political Alienation," *American Political Science Review*, 64 (June 1970), pp. 389–410; William Gamson, *Power and Discontent* (Homewood, Ill.: Dorsey Press, 1968); John E. Horton and Wayne E. Thompson, "Powerlessness and Political Negativism: A Study of Defeated Local Referendums," *American Journal of Sociology*, 67 (March 1962), pp. 485–492; Murray B. Levin and Murray Eden, "Political Strategy for the Alienated Voter," *Public Opinion Quarterly*, 26 (Spring 1962), pp. 47–63; Murray B. Levin, *The Alienated Voter* (New York: Holt, Rinehart and Winston, 1962); Edward L. McDill and Jeanne Claire Ridley, "Status, Anomia, Political Alienation, and Political Participation," *American Journal of Sociology*, 68 (September 1962), pp. 205–213; Marvin E. Olsen, "Two Categories of Political Alienation," *Social Forces*, 47 (March 1969), pp. 288–299; Arnold Rose, "Alienation and Participation: A Comparison of Group Leaders and the 'Mass,' " *American Sociological Review*, 27 (December 1962), pp. 834–838; Melvin Seeman, "On the Meaning of Alienation," *American Sociological Review*, 24 (December 1959), pp. 783–791; Fredric Templeton, "Alienation and Political Participation; Some Research Findings," *Public Opinion Quarterly*, 30 (Summer 1966), pp. 249–261; and Wayne E. Thompson and John E. Horton, "Political Alienation as a Force in Political Action," *Social Forces*, 38 (March 1960), pp. 190–195.

2. In addition to Aberbach, "Alienation and Political Behavior," and Finifter, "Dimensions of Political Alienation," also see Arthur G. Neal and Saloman Rettig, "Dimensions of Alienation among Manual and Non-Manual Workers," *American Sociological Review*, 28 (August 1963), p. 604; Arthur G. Neal and Saloman Rettig, "On the Multidimensionality of Alienation," *American Sociological*

Review, 32 (February 1967), pp. 54–64; and J. L. Simmons, "Some Intercorrelations Among 'Alienation' Measures," *Social Forces,* 44 (March 1966), pp. 370–372. The results are not fully consistent across studies and appear to depend partially on the specific measures used. Depending upon the method of analysis and the purposes for which it is used, the results sometimes can support both the unidimensional and multidimensional interpretations. Two studies, for example, supporting the single-dimension view and reporting moderate correlations (.41 to .65) between different dimensions are by Dean, "Alienation: Its Meaning and Measurement," p. 753, and by Olsen, "Two Categories of Political Alienation," p. 293.

3. Seeman and his associates have found this relationship to hold in studies in both political and nonpolitical settings: Melvin Seeman, "Alienation and Social Learning in a Reformatory," *American Journal of Sociology,* 69 (November 1963), pp. 270–284; Melvin Seeman, "Alienation, Membership and Political Knowledge: A Comparative Study," *Public Opinion Quarterly,* 30 (Fall 1966), pp. 353–367; Melvin Seeman "On the Personal Consequences of Alienation in Work," *American Sociological Review,* 32 (April 1967), pp. 273–285; and Melvin Seeman and John W. Evans, "Alienation and Learning in a Hospital Setting," *American Sociological Review* 27 (October 1962), pp. 772–781. Election studies in the United States also support this finding showing that the relationship between efficacy and participation is positive even when the effects of income and education are controlled, despite the fact that efficacy is even more highly associated with the demographic variables. John Robinson, Jerrold G. Rusk, and Kedra B. Head, *Measures of Political Attitudes* (Ann Arbor: Institute for Social Research, 1968), pp. 459 and 490. Erbe is one author who casts some doubt on this finding and concludes that "alienation is of some importance as a predictor [of participation] at the zero order, but higher order partialing raised grave doubt as to whether alienation affects political participation independently of socio-economic status and organizational involvement." Erbe, "Social Involvement and Political Activity," p. 213.

4. Several writers have tied changes in feelings of powerlessness to changes in levels of modernization and development. Daniel Lerner suggests that as individuals develop a sense of empathy, and can imagine themselves in someone else's place, they learn to conceptualize the world in terms of alternatives. Daniel Lerner, *The Passing of Traditional Society* (Glencoe, Ill.: Free Press, 1958). David Apter sees modernization as the development of social and political systems that increase the range of individual choices, and at the individual level, the perception that these choices are available. David Apter, *The Politics of Modernization* (Chicago: University of Chicago Press, 1965). Several studies have attributed the existence of such beliefs to particular child training practices that are common in some settings. Where punishment is capricious and arbitrary from the point of view of the young child, feelings of lack of control are likely to be manifest in the political realm. Pye sees these practices as the origins of the inability of Burmese politicians and administrators to make effective decisions, while Banfield considers it a root of the "amoral familism" of southern, rural Italy, where the possibility of meaningful cooperative activity is rejected outside the family. Lucien Pye, *Politics, Personality, and Nation Building* (New Haven: Yale University Press, 1962); and Edward Banfield, *The Moral Basis of a Backward Society* (New York: Free Press, 1958).

5. Aberbach, "Alienation and Political Behavior," pp. 93–98.

6. Finifter, "Dimensions of Political Alienation," pp. 397–406.

7. Finifter, ibid., pp. 406–409.

8. Among the antiwar activists Keniston interviewed in the United States, a high

sense of political efficacy is combined with their rejection of government leaders and their policies to produce a high political involvement. Kenneth Keniston, *The Young Radicals* (New York: Harcourt Brace and World, 1967).

9. This is shown, for example, in studies of local referenda in the United States. Local referenda, unlike most elections, provide an opportunity whereby feelings of political alienation can be translated into either "an undirected vote of resentment or an organized vote of opposition." Thompson and Horton, "Political Alienation as a Force in Political Action," p. 190. Participation is negatively related to political alienation in these situations, but there is a much stronger relationship between the direction of the vote and feelings of alienation, as those people who are the most alienated show the greatest tendency to cast negative votes on these issues. Thompson and Horton, ibid., McDill and Ridley, "Status, Anomia, Political Alienation, and Political Participation."

10. The more commonly cited mass society theorists include Hannah Arendt, *The Origins of Totalitarianism* (New York: Meridian, 1958); Daniel Bell, "The Theory of Mass Society," in Daniel Bell, *The End of Ideology* (Glencoe, Ill.: Free Press, 1960); Eric Hoffer, *The True Believer* (New York: Harper and Bros., 1951); William Kornhauser, *The Politics of Mass Society* (Glencoe, Ill.: Free Press, 1959); Robert Nisbet, *Community and Power* (New York: Oxford University Press, 1962); and Philip Selznick, "Institutional Vulnerability in Mass Society," in Philip Olson (ed.), *America as a Mass Society* (New York: Free Press, 1963).

11. The specific manner in which this is likely to occur is subject to great debate in the literature. Kornhauser provides a particularly clear statement of the two major points of view. The 'aristocratic' argument, he says, focuses on the development of elites by the masses, while the 'democratic' criticism is concerned with the manipulation of the mass by power-hungry elites. He contends that both perspectives must be integrated for a proper understanding of mass society, which is a condition where both elites and masses are vulnerable. Kornhauser, *The Politics of Mass Society*, passim.

12. Kornhauser, ibid., p. 212. The responses of the alienated are not necessarily abnormal or pathological as is often implied or even stated. One difficulty with many mass society theorists, such as Kornhauser, is that they are overly committed to an idealized conception of pluralistic democratic politics, which according to Gusfield "fails to give adequate weight to barriers which conflicts of interest offer to political harmony and compromise under any political structure." He then points out four types of situations where this is likely to take place. Joseph Gusfield, "Mass Society and Extremist Politics," *American Sociological Review*, 27 (February 1962), p. 20. The mass society theorists have been primarily concerned with the weaknesses of democratic regimes in the west in the twentieth century. Their analysis, however, as apart from the normative elements in their theory, applies quite well to phenomena such as independence movements in Africa and Asia as well.

13. Samuel Eldersveld, *Political Parties: A Behavioral Analysis* (Chicago: Rand McNally, 1964), Chapters 3, 7; and Donald Matthews, *The Social Background of Political Decision Makers* (Garden City, N.Y.: Doubleday, 1954).

14. Luther P. Gerlach and Virginia H. Hines, *People, Power, Change: Movements of Social Transformation* (Indianapolis and New York: Bobbs-Merrill, 1970), Chapters 3–4; John Lofland and Rodney Stark, "Becoming a World Saver: A Theory of Conversion to a Deviant Perspective," in Barry McLaughlin (ed.), *Studies in Social Movements* (New York: Free Press, 1969); and Charles Elder, "The 'Totalitarians' in Totalitarianism" (mimeo, n.d.).

15. Soloman E. Asch, "Effects of Group Pressure upon the Modificational Distortion

of Judgments," in Harold Guetzkow (ed.), *Groups, Leadership and Men* (Pittsburgh: University of Pittsburgh Press, 1951); Soloman E. Asch, "Studies of Independence and Conformity: I. A Minority of One Against a Unanimous Majority," *Psychological Monographs*, 70, No. 9, 1965; and Soloman E. Asch, "Issues on the Study of Social Influence on Judgment," in I. A. Berg and B. M. Bass (ed.), *Conformity and Deviation* (New York: Harper, 1961).

16. For an elaboration of this argument with reference to the United States and possibly other polities as well, see Murray Edelman, *The Symbolic Uses of Politics* (Urbana: University of Illinois Press, 1964); and Murray Edelman, *Politics as Symbolic Action* (Chicago: Markham Publishing Co., 1971).

17. Adam Przeworski and Henry Teune discuss the importance of trying to replace proper names with variable names in developing generalizations about social and political life. See their book, *The Logic of Comparative Social Inquiry* (New York: John Wiley & Sons, Inc., 1970), pp. 3–30. For an effort to apply the Przeworski-Teune method more systematically to these data, see Marc Howard Ross, "Political Participation, Alienation and Ethnicity: An African Case," *American Journal of Political Science*, 19 (May 1975).

Chapter 9

1. Pinard points out that mass society theorists stress the restraining effects of secondary and primary groups, but that it is also reasonable to stress their mobilizing effects, which are very likely to occur in a society with severe strain. Maurice Pinard, "Mass Society and Political Movements: A New Formulation," *American Journal of Sociology*, 73 (May 1968), p. 682.

2. Thomas Weisner reports that in a sample of Baluhya men in Nairobi matched with rural counterparts he found that the degree of urban experience (measured in years in the city) was no different for the two groups. The men in both his urban and rural samples, he contends, are continually moving back and forth between city and country depending upon employment opportunities, family obligations, and personal desires. See Thomas S. Weisner, "One Family, Two Households: A Rural-Urban Network Model of Urbanism" (Nairobi: University College, 1969).

3. Richard L. Sklar, *Nigerian Political Parties: Power in an Emergent African Nation* (Princeton, N.J.: Princeton University Press, 1963), pp. 481–482.

4. Donald Rothchild, "Ethnic Inequalities in Kenya," *Journal of Modern African Studies*, 7 (1969), p. 692:

5. Milton M. Gordon, *Assimilation in American Life: The Role of Race, Religion and National Origins* (New York: Oxford University Press, 1964).

6. Sklar asserts that the two principles, ethnicity and class, are inconsistent, ". . . the former implying a conception of the community as corporate and functionally integrated, while the latter signifies the fragmentation or division of the community into groups of conflicting (perceived) interests." Sklar, *Nigerian Political Parties*, p. 477. Nevertheless, empirical reality violates Sklar's logic.

7. An elaboration of this problem is found in Marc Howard Ross, "Class and Ethnic Bases of Political Mobilization in African Cities," in William John Hanna, *The Quality of Urban Life* (Miami, Fla.: University of Miami Press, 1975).

Index

Age
  distribution in Nairobi, 24, 52
  and education, 53–54
  and political participation, 162n
Alienation, 2, 4, 5, 7, 116
  and political participation, 117–125,
    126–128
  unidimensionality of, 117–118, 127,
    161n, 163–164n
arap Moi, Daniel, 67
Austin, Dennis, 102–103, 105

Bell, Wendell, 40

Churches, 57
  attendance of in Nairobi, 50–51
  in Shauri Moyo, 32, 34
Clignet, Remi, 108

Detribalization, 57, 67, 68, 70

Education, 36
  and ethnicity, 68–70
  as an investment, 53
  and life-style, 54–55
  and postindependence attitudes, 82–83
  and powerlessness, 94
  and rural-urban contact, 48
Efficacy, political. See Powerlessness,
    political
Epstein, A. L., 64–65
Estrangement, 4, 87–92, 118–119
  and ethnicity, 88
  and independence-style participation,
    120–121, 122–123
  index of, 160n
  and land ownership, 90
  and postindependence attitudes, 95–96
  and postindependence-style participa-
    tion, 120–123
  and powerlessness, 95–96, 124
Ethclass, 68, 135
Ethnicity, 5, 6, 9, 12, 18, 21, 50
  defining, 56–65
  and education, 68–70
  and estrangement, 88, 121
  and friendship choices, 67, 132
  and income, 68–70
  and political identification, 63–67, 71,
    132–133
  and political participation, 102

and politics, 56–73
and postindependence attitudes, 86–87
and powerlessness, 94–95
and rural-urban contact, 129
and social class, 72–73, 133–137
and social integration, 71–72
and voluntary associations, 162–163

Family structure
  in Kariokor, 35–37
  in Shauri Moyo, 35–37
Finifter, Ada, 117–118
Formal organizations. See Voluntary
    associations
Friendship choices, 50
  in the city, 132
  and education, 68–70
  and ethnicity, 67, 132
  and income, 68–70
  in Kariokor, 38
  and political participation, 106–108
  and sex and political participation,
    114–115
  and voluntary associations, 111

Gans, Herbert, 61
Glazer, Nathan, 64
Gluckman, Max, 62
Gordon, Milton, 135

Income, 35, 36
  and ethnicity, 68–70
  and life-style, 54–55
  and postindependence attitudes, 82–83
  and powerlessness, 94
  and rural-urban contact, 48–49, 130
  and wife's residence, 41
Independence-style participation, 101
  and estrangement, 12–21, 122–123
  and friendship choices, 106–108
  and political information, 109–110
  and powerlessness, 119–120, 121–122,
    123
  and rural-urban contact, 105–106
  and social status, 102–104
  and urban residence, 104–105
  and voluntary associations, 112–113
Information, political, 109–110
  and postindependence-style participa-
    tion, 109–110
  and sex differences, 140–141